THE TEACHINGS OF HASIDISM

D0140968

Library of Jewish Studies

THE TEACHINGS OF
HASIDISM

Edited, with introduction and notes, by JOSEPH DAN

with the assistance of ROBERT J. MILCH

BEHRMAN HOUSE, INC. | PUBLISHERS

Library of Congress Cataloging in Publication Data
Main entry under title:
The Teachings of Hasidism
  (Library of Jewish Studies; 9)
  Bibliography: p.
1. Hasidism—History—Sources. I. Dan, Joseph, 1935–   II. Series.
BM198.T4   1983   296.8′33   82-14688
ISBN 0-87441-346-X

© Copyright 1983 by Joseph Dan
Published by Behrman House, Inc., 235 Watchung Ave., West Orange, N.J. 07052
Manufactured in the United States of America

10 9 8 7 6 5 4 3

CONTENTS

PART TWO: THE ZADDIK   71

PART THREE: THE RELIGIOUS LIFE   101

PREFACE

IN THE LAST few decades there has been a growing interest in the ideas, the history, and the literature of Hasidism. Many anthologies of Hasidic writings have appeared in English and other languages. Various aspects of Hasidism have been described in detail by scholars and popular writers alike. Unfortunately, however, most of the anthologies are of material selected from secondary sources, or consist of modern, "literary" adaptations of original material, or concentrate on the most accessible (usually later) texts. The works written by early Hasidic rabbis, in the *classical* period of the movement (1780-1811), are not to be found in English translation. The common image of the Hasidic movement is, therefore, incomplete and inaccurate.

There is no way of changing this situation dramatically, because these original sources are really impossible to translate. Their basic literary characteristic is their use of the Hebrew homiletical method (*darshanut*); each passage is given over to an analysis, according to a special interpretative system, of several biblical verses, to which rabbinic sayings and very often medieval commentaries are added. The prevailing terminology is kabbalistic, and the reasoning—esoteric. An accurate scholarly translation of a page from the very first Hasidic book, *Toledot Ya'akov Yosef*, would require ten pages of notes, explanations, and comments in order to be understood. Because of this, many modern writers on Hasidism prefer to use other later sources, and mainly narrative works (the earliest being *In Praise of the Besht*, published in 1815, a generation after *Toledot Ya'akov Yosef*, which was published in 1780). Thus the classical period and classical works remain relatively neglected.

The present anthology offers the English reader a selection of texts from the classical period. The passages have been chosen for the importance of the ideas they express and also because they are representative of the thought of the individual author. The choice of selections has in part been governed by the desire to avoid passages heavily burdened with homiletical formulations or detailed kabbalistic discussions. Kabbalistic terminology has been kept to the minimum required for accuracy. The main goal has been to present the most significant works of early Hasidism on the central themes that preoccupied the first Hasidic rabbis.

The Hasidic writers used a limited Hebrew vocabulary (aside from the numerous quotations from the Bible and other texts with which their works abound). Some of the most important works were preserved only in the form of notes taken by disciples as they listened to their rabbi preaching; these include the works of Rabbi Dov Baer (the Maggid of Mezherich) and of Rabbi Nahman of Bratslav. An accurate translation must reflect the nature of the original, with its limited vocabulary and its constantly recurring phrases. This may make the text seem rather thin, linguistically, but in the present translation accuracy has been the first consideration, and no attempt has been made artificially to "elevate" the language of the sources.

It is my belief that an encounter with original Hasidic thought, in a form which reflects the original as closely as possible, will reveal the enormous strength of this religious school, which made it a dominant power in Jewish life in the last two centuries.

It is my pleasant obligation to acknowledge the invaluable editorial aid of Robert J. Milch, who not only transformed my own English into better English, but in his reworking of the translations succeeded in capturing the spirit of these Hasidic texts while remaining faithful to the letter. The result, I hope, has been to make the teachings of the Hasidic rabbis as readable as they are instructive and illuminating.

Joseph Dan
Mount Scopus, Jerusalem

INTRODUCTION

I

THE BEGINNINGS OF the Hasidic movement can be dated accurately only in conjunction with a definition of the essence and meaning of Hasidism. Those who maintain that Hasidism began with the first public appearance of Rabbi Israel Ba'al Shem Tov—the year 1736 according to Hasidic tradition—also maintain in effect that Hasidism is preeminently a religious movement founded by Rabbi Israel, and that his activities constitute its earliest history. Unfortunately, however, we have little reliable information about the theology of the Besht, as Rabbi Israel is generally known, and thus it is extremely difficult to prove that the basic elements of later Hasidism were found in his teachings.

Another possible date for the beginning of Hasidism is 1760, when the Besht died and was succeeded by his disciple, Rabbi Dov Baer, the Maggid (Preacher) of Mezherich. Accepting this date reflects the idea that Hasidism was first and foremost a social phenomenon—an organized mass movement, based on the Maggid's court, that was intended to conquer and transform Jewish society. This view, however, also presents difficulties. Later Hasidism was characterized by the notion of the Zaddik and by the simultaneous existence of several Zaddikim, each with his own court and disciples, but the Zaddik concept was not instituted or systematically formulated during the Maggid's lifetime. Moreover, while the Maggid's court provided the necessary basis for the organizational growth of Hasidism, and in some respects the Maggid conducted himself like a Zaddik, the concept is not found in his teachings. In any case, he was the sole leader of Hasidism in his day, while later Hasidism was subdivided into several sects or groupings, each headed by its own Zaddik.

The period in which Hasidism could be regarded as having one leader ended around 1772 with the Maggid's death. His best disciples soon began to establish their own Hasidic courts, creating a multi-centered movement. All of these former followers of the Maggid played similar leadership roles, setting up independent *edot*, or congregations. Rabbi Shneur Zalman of Lyady (1745–1812), the founder of Habad Lubavitch Hasidism, for instance, was one of the Maggid's younger disciples. Rabbi Menahem Mendel of Vitebsk (1730–1788), who migrated to Eretz Yisrael in 1777 and established a small but influential congregation in the Galilee, was one of the older and more prominent disciples. Rabbi Elimelech of Lyzhansk (1717–1787), Rabbi Levi Yitzhak of Berdichev (1740–1810), and many others also established Hasidic congregations. Some of them soon had thousands of followers, and in some instances their courts continued to exist for many generations. Hasidism now began rapidly to assume the social and ideological characteristics that were to be its main contribution to Jewish life in the nineteenth century and afterward.

The new Hasidic courts, as the setting where the theories concerning the role of the Zaddik took root and flourished, gave a firm ideological basis to the emerging Hasidic social institutions. As a result, the year 1772, when all of these developments can be said to have begun, is sometimes reckoned as the date of the movement's true beginnings. There is another reason for favoring this date. In 1772, the rabbis of Vilna and other major centers of Jewish learning first took drastic steps *against* Hasidism, initiating a controversy that raged for generations and split East European Jewry—the world's largest concentration of Jews—into two opposing camps. The struggle was fierce and sometimes took on a very bitter aspect, especially when the tsarist authorities in Russia were asked to intervene, a step which resulted in the imprisonment of several Hasidic leaders. Because of this bitter conflict, the emerging Hasidic movement became one of the most important items on the Jewish ideological agenda.

Despite these considerations, however, there is good reason to prefer not 1772 but 1780 as the date when the Hasidic movement really began. In Judiasm ideas spread more through the power of the written word than by any other means, and a major Jewish religious phenomenon without a literature is well-nigh unthinkable. It was in 1780, with the publication of the *Toledot Ya'akov Yosef*, a compilation of sayings by the founder of Hasidism, as edited by Rabbi Ya'akov Yosef of Polonnoye (d. ca. 1782), that the emerging Hasidic movement obtained its first authoritative text. Even today this major collection of the Besht's homilies, compiled by one of his disciples, is the chief source for understanding early Hasidic thought. It was followed in rapid succession by many other works, among them two additional books by Rabbi Ya'akov Yosef, Rabbi Dov Baer's *Maggid Devarav Le'Ya'akov*, the *Noam Elimelech* by Rabbi Elimelech of Lyzhansk, and Rabbi Shneur Zalman's *Tania*. By the early years of the nineteenth century Hasidism could boast a sizable library whose volumes reflected its diverse ideological trends.

While Hasidism undoubtedly existed as a social and historical force before 1780, it did not come into its own as a movement exercising significant theological influence until its first theological works were published and circulated. The formative period of Hasidic theology and literature, during which these works took root in Jewish thought, extended from 1780 to 1815. Roughly coinciding with the Napoleonic Wars, this period of about four decades was marked by a series of internal changes that brought about the beginning of a new era in the evolution of Hasidism.

The Hasidic writings dating from the years between 1780 and 1815 almost all belong to a single literary genre, the exegetical homily, and thus are characterized by the structural features and internal conventions of the sermon. Most of them, in fact, were based on sermons actually preached by their authors, and in many cases they were first put into writing by disciples who took notes when the sermons were delivered, sometimes producing different versions of the same homily. The influence of the sermonic genre can be detected even in the few works from this period that are not predominantly homiletical in character, Rabbi Shneur Zalman's *Tania* and the *Zava'at Ha-Rivash* and *Keter Shem Tov*, two collections of the Besht's sayings.

Rabbi Shneur Zalman, like all the Zaddikim of his own and later generations, expressed himself primarily through the medium of homilies, and his major works, especially the voluminous

Likutey Torah, are clearly homiletical in character. The *Tania,* formally an ethical work in a Hebrew literary tradition that began in the eleventh and twelfth centuries and was revitalized in the sixteenth, especially in Safed, by the emergence of a kabbalistic ethical literature, also has sermonic qualities, as did the *Reshit Hochmah* ("The Source of Wisdom") of Rabbi Elijah de Vidas, perhaps the most important of the kabbalistic ethical works.[1] As I. Tishby has demonstrated, however, both the original and later versions of the *Tania* were designed to present Rabbi Shneur Zalman's ideas in an esoteric form whose full meaning would be apparent to an inner circle but not to the general reading public.[2]

Sermonic influence is also evident in the *Zava'at Ha-Rivash* and the *Keter Shem Tov.* Both of these collections of sayings by the Besht were compiled in the late eighteenth century in response to the Hasidic movement's need for authentic writings by its founder that would be easier to read and understand than the larger homiletical collections already being circulated. Though made up of relatively short, independent pericopes rather than long sermons, the *Zava'at Ha-Rivash* and *Keter Shem Tov* clearly belong to the homiletical genre. Most of the pericopes in the two collections, taken mainly from the larger works of Rabbi Ya'akov Yosef and the Maggid, provide exegetical interpretations of biblical verses or talmudic sayings, and this seems to accord with what little we know about the Besht's teaching techniques. It was apparently his practice to give homilies on the weekly Torah reading or some other biblical passage. While the complete texts of his sermons were eventually lost, his disciples remembered the highlights and incorporated them in their own works. The compilers of the collected sayings, in turn, separated these materials from their new settings and presented them as independent pericopes.

In passing, it should be emphasized that the famous "Hasidic stories" that typify Hasidic literature for many present-day readers did not come into being until long after the period under discussion. Moreover, their place in Hasidism has been exaggerated to the point of distorting the historical picture. Only two narrative works were published during the whole first century of Hasidism— the *Shivhey Ha-Besht*[3] and the *Stories* of Rabbi Nahman of Bratslav—and both of these appeared in 1815, more than half a century after the death of the Besht and thirty-five years after Hasidism began producing its extensive homiletical literature. Another two generations passed before the next collection of Hasidic stories was published in 1863.

When such collections finally began to appear with some frequency, they were invariably written by individuals who were not Hasidim, but either former members of the movement or adherents of the Haskalah (Enlightenment), and the motives of the authors were primarily pecuniary. Thus, the "Hasidic story" is to a great extent a twentieth-century fantasy created by writers who overemphasized a literary form that they found more satisfying than the movement's authentic literature. If we are to achieve a true perspective on early Hasidic teachings, we must leave these distorted modern outpourings behind.[4]

The crucial role of the sermonic form in early Hasidic literature was related to certain aspects of the religious, social, and cultural milieu of East European Jewry in the era when Hasidism began shaping itself. The sermon was Jewry's primary and sometimes only means of communicating new religious ideas (with the exception of ideas of purely halakhic significance). New ideas were carried from place to place mainly by the numerous itinerant preachers of the day. Even more important, the sermon delivered by the synagogue preacher, whether an itinerant or an official functionary of the community, if it could afford one, was the only medium through which new ideas were regularly expounded and explained to the Jewish lay public.

The influence of the ideas conveyed in this manner was enhanced by the inherent conservatism of the sermonic form. While it was a basic premise of any sermon that the preacher had something new to say, since otherwise he would remain silent rather than expose himself to adverse criticism, the message of the sermon was built upon a series of interpretive quotations from the Bible, the Talmud, and other authoritative sources, thereby seemingly confirming the accepted view that everything worth knowing was already embodied in the sacred texts. The preacher, in effect, was not presenting innovations but simply plumbing the depths of the tradition and uncovering ideas that had always been there for those who knew how to find them.

In this and other respects, the sermonic form was exactly what the emerging Hasidic movement needed. The homiletical technique of working Hasidic ideas into interpretations of the traditional texts made it unnecessary for the movement, during its formative stages, to define itself too precisely by categorically specifying what it accepted from the older sources and what it rejected. In addition, the sermonic approach—together with other factors, of course—

helped to preserve the religious orthodoxy of Hasidism during its early generations. Most important, however, the use of the sermon made a tremendous contribution to the success of Hasidism among the uneducated masses, for whom the sermon was the only means of coming to grips with issues of religious import.

It would be wrong, however, to say that Hasidism consciously chose to exploit the sermonic form. Many of the early Hasidic teachers were originally itinerant preachers by profession, wandering from one community to another and preaching in the synagogue for the price of a Sabbath meal, and it was only natural for them to use the exegetical homily as a means of articulating their beliefs.[5] While it is true that Hasidism was the first and probably the only major religious movement in Jewish history to rely so exclusively on the sermonic genre, this simply demonstrates that it began among a class that had never before produced a major religious phenomenon. Prior to the advent of Hasidism, new religious movements had been founded by settled thinkers who formulated their ideas in theological treatises, whether philosophical or kabbalistic. Popular preachers incorporated the new teachings in their sermons only after a movement had begun to win wide acceptance, and as a result homiletical literature generally played a role only in the later stages when the expanding new religious movement began to percolate down to the masses. In the case of Hasidism, however, the process was turned around, for the masses were the very segment of the populace in which it began and first took hold.

II

IN THE ERA preceding the emergence of Hasidism, Jewish culture went through a great metamorphosis along kabbalistic lines. As part of this development, which reached its culmination in the Palestinian town of Safed in the sixteenth century, the orientation of Hebrew homiletical literature—indeed of all Jewish popular literature—was transformed. Previously primarily rabbinic or philosophical in outlook, it now became almost totally kabbalistic. More or less concurrently, the kabbalistic philosophical system of Rabbi Isaac Luria Ashkenazi of Safed (1534–1572), known as Ha-Ari,[6] gained a position of preeminence so pervasive that it provided the basis for virtually every school of thought in Judaism from around 1700 until well into the nineteenth century (and even today in some Orthodox circles).

Given this intellectual and spiritual climate, Hasidism could hardly have avoided coming under the influence of the Kabbalah. In many respects, Hasidism revived kabbalistic notions that had fallen into desuetude. In addition it derived its fundamental ideas and theological terminology from the Kabbalah. This does not mean, however, that all Hasidim or all Zaddikim were either mystics or kabbalists. It would be more accurate to say that there were mystical elements in the thought of several outstanding Hasidic teachers, but that these never became essential parts of the Hasidic world-view.

To cite an example, the disciples of the Maggid of Mezherich, among them the founders of the main Hasidic sects, did not, for the most part, accept the quietistic personal mysticism that is evident in their teacher's sermons.[7] Moreover, since the Maggid's mysticism cannot be said with any certainty to have derived from the Besht's teachings, it must be regarded, at least in part, as a personal attitude toward the world and God that was not necessarily shared by those who accepted his leadership and many other elements of his doctrine.

Much the same applies to Rabbi Nahman of Bratslav (1772–1811). Other Hasidic teachers rejected his intense messianic mysticism and subsequently excommunicated and persecuted his followers, this being one of the reasons why the Bratslav sect was for a long time so small. Similarly, while several Hasidic teachers devoted considerable talent and effort to kabbalistic studies, there was a disjunction of sorts between their kabbalistic interests and their Hasidism, as we can best see, perhaps, from the example of Rabbi Yitzhak Izik Safrin of Komarno (1806–1874), a prolific writer and scholar, and the leader of an important Hasidic sect, whose five-volume exegesis of the Zohar, overwhelmingly kabbalistic in orientation, displays almost no trace of distinctively Hasidic ideas.

While Hasidism's view of the world, then, was unavoidably shaped and colored by the Kabbalah and its mystical doctrines, Hasidism was not fundamentally mystical in the usual sense of the word. The reason for this is not hard to determine. Hasidism was a mass movement, but the mystical stance is intensely individualistic and cannot easily be maintained in a formally structured group setting, at least not for long. As a result, the mystical tendencies associated with the Kabbalah inevitably became more generalized as they gained wide popular acceptance, and this was happening even before the emergence of Hasidism. By the same token, as kabbalistic terms and concepts became an integral part of the Jewish spiritual vocabulary, a development to which Hasidism made an immense contribution, much of their original force was diluted. In consequence, the Kabbalah that animated Hasidism is best described not as a process that transformed every believer into a mystic but as a collective spiritual attitude toward the world, history, and God.

Inasmuch as generalizations are possible, the kabbalistic ideas utilized by Hasidism derived from two main sources: the sefirot doctrine of the Zohar (written in Spain in the thirteenth century), and Rabbi Isaac Luria's doctrine of *zimzum, shevirah,* and *tikkun*. Most of the Hasidic teachers preferred the older, somewhat simpler conceptualization of the sefirot found in the Zohar to the more complicated Lurianic system as developed by Rabbi Hayim Vital, Luria's disciple, but they did accept Luria's cosmic history and many of his other revolutionary ideas, although not without introducing modifications, either their own or taken from earlier treatments of the Lurian theology.

The sefirot doctrine, one of the most fundamental expressions of kabbalistic mysticism, is based on the belief that the infinite Godhead—called Ein Sof[8] and described in terms similar to those used by Maimonides and his disciples in describing the philosophical Godhead—emanated a series of ten powers, or sefirot,[9] each with its own specific characteristics and functions; and that these ten powers, which are completely divine but have limits because they exist in time, can be described by means of mystical symbolism. Stated so baldly, this system is not inherently mystical and in fact resembles the rationalist systems expounded by several medieval Neoplatonic philosophers. It became a mystical system with the introduction of the view that the sefirot were dynamic rather than static.

In the kabbalistic literature as a whole, and especially in the richly detailed Zohar, the sefirot were intensely personalized. Going far beyond simple descriptions of the functions of the various sefirot, a lavishly imaginative symbolism was used to depict the individual characteristics of each sefirah in extensive detail, so much so that kabbalists came to see each one as a distinct personal entity. Hundreds of different symbols were used in these descriptions, especially in discussing Tiferet, the sixth sefirah, and Shekhinah, the tenth and last. Tiferet, the masculine element in the divine world, was the central power among the *sefirot ha-binyan*—the "sefirot of construction" which created the world and guided its destiny—while Shekhinah, its feminine counterpart, was the divine element closest to man and thus the subject of a large part of human religious endeavor as well as the first possible contact of a mystic ascending to the divine world.[10]

With the publication and circulation of the Zohar, the cosmological system of the sefirot—conceiving the world of the sefirot as the mystical pleroma, the "fullness" of divine powers comprising the Godhead—became the Kabbalah's most obvious and recognizable "trademark." Hasidic theology completely accepted this system, which forms the basis for almost every Hasidic theological statement and exegetical pericope. But in doing so Hasidism had to disregard a more recent development in the conceptualization of the sefirot— a new system that had emerged from the Lurianic school in Safed.

III

THE LURIANIC KABBALAH is a radical cosmic myth which was formulated by the great visionary and mystic Rabbi Isaac Luria (1534–1572) and reduced to theological terms by his foremost associate, Rabbi Hayim Vital (1542–1620). It was developed among a circle of a dozen or so disciples in Safed, the main center of kabbalistic and mystic studies in the sixteenth century. Luria's system had very little influence during his lifetime, even in Safed. After his death, Vital swore most of the other disciples to silence about the master's doctrines and also tried to keep secret his own voluminous writings on the subject. Even a generation later, not a word about Luria's doctrines is found in letters from Safed that otherwise offer many details about his life, personal practices, disciples, and related matters. Within another twenty years, however, the situation had completely changed; the revolutionary new revelations from Safed had, in effect, taken the Jewish world by storm, and for the next two centuries Luria's system totally dominated Jewish religious thought and culture.

Though subsequent thinkers universally accepted the essential elements of Luria's cosmic myth, its many problematic and sometimes controversial aspects led them to introduce revisions of various kinds, some marginal, some of more substantial impact. Indeed, throughout the period in which the Lurian system was dominant, whether we are discussing the tiny kabbalistic circles of Italy, such as the school of Rabbi Joseph Ergas (1685–1730) or the more influential school of Rabbi Moses Hayim Luzzatto (1707–1746), or even major historical movements like Sabbatianism and Hasidism, it might well be said that Jewish thought was chiefly occupied by a confrontation or dialogue with Luria, a struggle to accept as much as possible from his teachings and to provide satisfactory substitutes for elements of his system deemed unacceptable. Deviations and modifications notwithstanding, Judaism as a whole, for the first time in more than a thousand years, was united in adherence to one theological system. The hidden power that enabled this system to win the minds of such a widely scattered people in so short a time will become apparent when we have discussed its mythic concepts in more detail.

First and foremost, the Lurianic Kabbalah was a messianic/ redemptive system which emphasized both the special role of the Jewish people in the divine order and the idea of the individual responsibility of each and every Jew for helping to perform Israel's God-given task. Though many of its ideas were strange or difficult, Luria's system won such wide acceptance because it addressed two basic questions that Jews have always asked, though perhaps more poignantly in the generations immediately preceding and following Luria's lifetime: Why is there an exile? and what is the meaning, or function, of the commandments in the Torah? In the course of answering these and many other questions in the great mythic tale at the heart of his kabbalistic system, Luria clearly pointed out the practical acts, both individual and national, that could liberate the Jewish people and bring about the universal redemption.

The central idea of the Lurianic Kabbalah is one which had been at best secondary in all previous Jewish philosophies: exile. Although the dispersion of world Jewry had begun long before the common era, and the destruction of the Second Temple in 70 C.E. had made exile the universal Jewish condition, even for those still living in the Land of Israel, Jewish thinkers before Luria had treated exile as a kind of aberration from the normal order of things, brought about by the Jews themselves—a deviation, caused by Jewish sins, from the original divine plan for a perfect world. In the era following the catastrophic expulsion from Spain (1492), which terminated the existence of what had once been world Jewry's most stable and prosperous exilic community, Jews were increasingly oppressed by a mounting sense of futility as well as a feeling of despair about the hardships and degradation of life as a minority among the gentile nations. Responding to the yearning for an explanation of Jewish suffering that would not shelve the question by blaming it on the failings of previous generations, Luria, unlike his predecessors, made exile the very basis of his conceptions of God, the world, man, and the people of Israel. In doing so he gave exile a far-reaching significance not simply for the Jewish people but for the divine order and the entire cosmos.

Luria's cosmic myth begins with a question pertaining to the system of sefirot described in the preceding section: At the moment when time and history began, God emanated from Himself something that was less than Himself even though it was a divine power (the sefirot). How was this possible, since until that moment God Himself comprised everything that was (or putting it differently, comprised nothingness, since as yet nothing existed) and thus there was no "outside" into which the Ein Sof could emanate entities that were not Ein Sof?

To this question Luria gave the following answer: The process of bringing into existence things that were not purely Ein Sof began with the withdrawal of the Ein Sof from some part of existence, which came into existence by virtue of that very withdrawal. The act of concentration, or contraction, by means of which the Ein Sof vacated a portion of itself, thereby making possible the creation of space and time, is called the zimzum (sometimes transliterated tsimtsum), a term that in midrashic usage had referred to the concentration of the Shekhinah, or Divine Presence, between the cherubim in the Temple. According to this conception, the history of existence, including divine existence, did not begin with a positive creative act by God but with the negative step of withdrawal or exile. In other words, the world came into being because God accepted exile from the space that was thus created.

The introduction into Jewish thought of an idea so sweeping and fecund on the problem of exile made all previous discussions of the subject seem insufficient and shallow. The zimzum concept was widely adopted by the Hasidic teachers, sometimes with modifications. Even more important in Luria's treatment of exile, however, and described in far more elaborate mythic detail, was the second phase of his cosmic history, known as the *shevirat ha-kelim*, or "breaking of the vessels."

In this phase of the myth, which describes events that took place after the zimzum, the Ein Sof emanated divine lights, and these lights, going through a series of sequential steps, assumed the forms of the ten sefirot—or, putting it differently, flowed into "vessels" that were supposed to give them their sefirotic shapes and individuality. The process was never completed, however, because the vessels could not, or would not, hold the lights flowing into them and suddenly broke. As a result, the shattered pieces of the vessels, with isolated fragments of divine light (termed *nizonot,* or "sparks") clinging to them, fell downward, while the remaining lights ascended back toward the Ein Sof.

Luria's explanation of this cosmic catastrophe marks one of the decisive differences between his system and previous kabbalistic philosophies.[11] Earlier thinkers had suppressed or deemphasized the dualism implicit in the Kabbalah, but Luria gave it full expression, and his stark, full-blown dualism provided the essential grounding for a cosmology that seemed a perfect reflection of the harsh realities of the history and daily existence of the homeless, persecuted Jewish people.[12]

According to Luria, the Ein Sof had originally embodied two potentially opposed powers. The process of zimzum and creation had been intended to resolve the differences between these powers, but one of them had refused to participate, thwarting the attempt at creation by precipitating the breaking of the vessels. Chaos ensued, and a dualistic world came into being in the empty space vacated by the zimzum. The rebellious powers occupied the lower part, creating a realm of evil, while the fragments of divine light that had managed to tear themselves away during the shevirah took refuge in the upper part. The nizonot that did not escape, however, were trapped in the lower space, and by their presence enabled the evil realm to prevail, for existence of any kind is impossible unless sustained by the power of the divine light, and the evil powers obtained the sustenance they required by "sucking" it from the imprisoned sparks.

The zimzum myth, the first phase of Luria's cosmic history, "dignified" exile by making it a cosmic principle and, in effect, a "given" of the world order rather than an aberration. The myth of the captive sparks gave the exile an immediate concrete significance in the life of every individual believer, because rescuing the trapped sparks, as will be explained below, was not only within the individual's power but a religious task that God had specifically entrusted to every single member of the Jewish people.

In the next phase of the myth, describing the sequel to the

shevirah, there was another outpouring of emanations from the Ein Sof. Since the evil elements were no longer involved in the process, there was no repetition of the shevirah, but even so the emanated sefirot, and the created worlds below them, were unable to achieve the required purity and thus could not assume their rightful stations. Perfect existence of any kind was impossible because the shevirah had affected the entire cosmos, and it would remain impossible unless and until the shevirah was mended.

The *tikkun*, or "mending" of what had been broken, was the most potent of the concepts that Luria's system brought into the forefront of the Jewish religious consciousness. According to Luria, man—that is to say, Jewish man, starting with Adam and including every Jew who has ever lived—was created for the express purpose of performing the tikkun. The whole course of Jewish history, from its very outset, was understood in terms of setbacks and advances in the attempt to perform the tikkun. Adam, for example, should have completed the tikkun but instead, because of his sin, brought about a catastrophic new shevirah in which more sparks were cast down into the realm of evil. Similarly, the whole people of Israel almost succeeded in completing the tikkun when they accepted the Torah Mount Sinai, but the sin of the golden calf caused yet another shevirah, and still more sparks fell into the clutches of the evil powers.

The task of performing the tikkun was assigned to man because the human being's dual nature—a divine soul within a body controlled by the evil powers—makes the life of each individual a reflection or enactment, writ small, of the situation in the cosmos as a whole, not merely in symbol or metaphor but in fact. The fate of all existence depends upon the outcome of the great struggle between good and evil, but the struggle is worked out in countless individual variations. A victory for good is scored whenever a human being defeats his evil impulses; the satanic powers win a victory and gain control of more sparks whenever a human being sins. The battlefield or focal point of the struggle, as it were, is the individual's observance of God's commandments as written in the Torah and elaborated in Jewish law and ethics. Every deed of every Jew takes place within this framework and decisively affects the overall conflict.

Luria's exposition of the cosmic struggle between good and evil, one of the most significant elements of his system to be adopted by Hasidism, had great importance for the everyday conduct of the believer, based on Luria's view that Torah, commandments, and precepts were inherently coordinated with the tikkun process. Since the commandments, the precepts, and the trapped sparks had all originated together in the divine world, each commandment and precept was regarded as having an intimate relationship to at least one of the imprisoned sparks. By making contact with a spark through the appropriate religious act (i.e., the commandment or precept specifically related to it), a human being can release the spark from imprisonment and restore it to its rightful place in the divine world. Since evil, like anything else, can only exist if it is able to obtain sustenance from the divine light, the complete separation that will result when all Jews uplift all the imprisoned nizonot will bring about the total abolition of evil itself, and, thus, the long-awaited final redemption.

In view of the fact that individual defeats would result in still more sparks falling into the satanic realm, head-on confrontations with evil were discouraged, and instead believers were urged to avoid temptation. On the other hand, since good deeds and properly performed commandments bring the redemption closer, believers were urged to dedicate their lives to performing both the religious acts traditionally prescribed by Jewish law and the innovative tikkunim (special practices and liturgical recitations) devised by Luria and his disciples.

IV

PRESENT-DAY ADMIRERS of Hasidism, inspired by a nostalgic regard for its ideas and organizational coherence and for the certainty and sense of rootedness of its adherents, are often unaware of the sobering fact that early Hasidism, especially in the 1770's, met with fierce and sometimes ruthless opposition from the greatest Jewish authorities of the time, most notably Rabbi Elijah, the Gaon of Vilna (1720–1797). Since the Hasidic movement's rabbinical adversaries, the Mitnaggedim, were unquestionably motivated by love for Israel and the Torah, we must ask why they failed to see Hasidism's great burning light and why they ignored (as some of their successors do even today) the profound new message it taught. This question cannot easily be put aside, but it cannot be answered without considering Hasidism's immediate historical background.

An East European rabbi in the 1770's would have been

unable to ignore the new movement's many similarities to the ill-fated Sabbatian movement, founded by the false messiah Shabbetai Zevi (1626–1676), which had swept the Jewish world in the latter half of the seventeenth century.[13] Though Sabbatianism had been discredited since 1666, when its founder converted to Islam, its repercussions were still felt, and it continued to exist in Poland, albeit in a grossly corrupted form, as recently as the last years of the Besht's lifetime. In 1757 and 1760, in Kamieniec and Lvov respectively, the Catholic authorities had organized public disputations between Jews and representatives of a Sabbatian sect headed by Jacob Frank (1726–1791). The anti-Jewish animus of the Frankist disputants was so vile that they had even professed to substantiate the notorious blood-libel accusation, a thoroughly baseless pretext for persecutions of the Jews since the Middle Ages, and in 1760 a large group of Frankists had converted to Christianity.

In our day, Hasidism is one of the strongest pillars of the most Orthodox branch of Judaism. Its dedication to Torah and the strict observance of the commandments is beyond doubt, and thus it is easy to conclude, two hundred years after the fact, that there was no basis for the fear that it would follow the same antinomian and heretical course taken by Sabbatianism. Things looked very different in 1772 though, and with the Frankist episode still fresh in their memories, many rabbis would have been suspicious of any new religious movement. And even beyond this understandable caution, there was much else in early Hasidism to give them real concern.

To begin with, Hasidism originated in Podolia and Volhynia, the geographic region that had been the main center of Sabbatianism in Eastern Europe, and the early Hasidic teachers came from the same social stratum in which Sabbatianism had spread—the class of impoverished, rootless, itinerant preachers, often lacking formal rabbinical education, who were the natural carriers of radical new ideas.[14] Moreover, just as Shabbetai Zevi himself had not begun his career with an outright denial of Jewish tradition but instead made some "minor" innovations, so too Hasidism had made a number of minor departures from accepted Jewish practice in regard to the time of prayer, conduct during prayer, ritual slaughter, and a few other matters.

Perhaps most important, Hasidism was, in a sense, a "people's movement" in a society whose leadership "establishment" comprised a kind of intellectual elite. By cultivating mass enthusiasm and religious spontanteity, sometimes in apparent contravention of accepted Torah norms, Hasidism seemed to be undermining the communal leadership role of the rabbis and halakhic scholars.[15] Since the social organization of European Jewry in this period depended solely on respect for the rabbis and voluntary submission to their authority as interpreters of the Torah, many members of the rabbinate feared an outbreak of the same kind of social and religious chaos that had come about when the Sabbatians refused to uphold the "old" Torah and preached a "new" Torah appropriate for the messianic era in which they supposed they were living.

While the Mitnaggedim rarely mentioned the traumatic Sabbatian experience in their writings, it is the only factor that can explain the ferocity of their attacks on the emerging Hasidic movement. Since the Hasidim, like all Jews of the time, were aware of Sabbatianism and familiar with its ideas, there was at least a basis for the suspicion that there might be a link of some kind between the two movements. Beyond this rather obvious observation, and the equally obvious points that Hasidism, unlike Sabbatianism, was not messianic or antinomian and never became a heresy, we must still ask whether Sabbatian ideas shaped Hasidism to any significant degree.

This is one of the most vexed questions about the early history of Hasidism, and in answering it we must note that there were several points of contact between the two movements. Perhaps best known is the fact that the Besht expressed sorrow about the conversion of the Frankists in 1760 and blamed this disaster on the rabbinical authorities.[16] In addition, early Hasidism certainly utilized the writings of Rabbi Ya'akov Kopel Lifshitz of Mezherich, a well-known Sabbatian,[17] as well as the *Hemdat Yamim*, an eighteenth-century homiletical work of Sabbatian origin that was sometimes attributed to Nathan of Gaza (1643–1680), the "prophet" who had been Shabbetai Zevi's closest associate.[18] Finally, as Gershom Scholem has suggested, the Besht himself may have been influenced by the *Sefer Ha-Zoref*, an esoteric Sabbatian work by Rabbi Heshel Zoref.[19]

Although several similar links could also be pointed out, the real question is whether Sabbatianism decisively influenced Hasidism at the historical and literary points where the two movements met. This cannot be determined from the links themselves. An answer will only emerge from a study of the fundamental ideas of Hasidism, especially the doctrines of the uplifting of the sparks and of the Zaddik, in the early period before these ideas came to the fore in the controversy between the Hasidim and the Mitnaggedim and served as the basis for accusations that Hasidism had Sabbatian leanings.

V

IN MANY RESPECTS, Hasidism began as a revivalist movement. Its characteristic doctrines, unlike those of the Lurianic Kabbalah, were neither original nor revolutionary, and many of them were revitalized versions of ideas that had long been part of Judaism. Joy in prayer and in the performance of religious precepts, love for the whole people of Israel and for the poor and ignorant, and opposition to dogmatic study of the Torah, for instance, all had the endorsement of longstanding Jewish tradition, while certain other ideas, perhaps more original, were expounded only by individuals and were never accepted by the Hasidic movement as a whole. Thus, the early Hasidic teachers, in all probability, saw themselves less as innovators than as restorers of neglected ideas to the forefront of Jewish religious consciousness. The conventionality of their teachings is reflected by their extensive reliance on the homiletical mode, although, as pointed out earlier, this technique could also be used to cloak new ideas in traditional garb.

Because of the complex interaction between old and new in Hasidic thought, it is often difficult to decide which early Hasidic doctrines were original and which were simply reemphasized or revived elements of the ethical and spiritual heritage that the Hasidim shared with all Jews. Criticism of the sterility of Talmud study, for example, abounds in Jewish literature as early as the medieval *Sefer Hasidim* and was renewed in Eastern Europe in the sixteenth and seventeenth centuries by the Maharal of Prague (Rabbi Judah Loew ben Bezalel, ca. 1525–1609), Rabbi Ephraim of Luntshits (1550–1619), and other scholars. The emphasis on joy in worship, which did not play a prominent role in Hasidic preaching or practice until the beginning of the nineteenth century,[20] is found in Hebrew ethical works from the thirteenth and, especially, the sixteenth centuries,[21] while advocacy of a benevolent attitude toward the ignorant, another late development in Hasidic history, also had deep roots in Jewish tradition.[22] Finally, love for the people of Israel pervades Jewish teachings in all eras and can hardly be described as the monopoly of any one sect.

The complex nature of the question of Hasidic originality is underscored by the Hasidic version of the zimzum concept. In the Lurian system, it will be recalled, the zimzum was a process occurring within the Godhead that expressed the exilic sensibility and reflected the great mythic struggle in the cosmic world. By describing how God separated Himself from certain of His own divine elements, which remained in the space vacated by the zimzum, the concept explained how and, to some extent, why it was possible for the world to be created. Hasidism offered a completely different explanation. In the Hasidic view, the zimzum was not caused by an internal struggle within the Godhead but by God's love for what was created, and thus it was not a self-exilic act of the Godhead but an expression of divine charity and love for mankind.

The Hasidic theory of the zimzum followed from a cosmology that differed from Luria's in many important particulars. The Hasidic teachers agreed that all existing things derived their existence from emanations of divine light from the Ein Sof, but they maintained that the divine light had been so intensely bright in its pristine form that its full power could not be endured and "filtering" was required before existence of any kind became possible. In consequence, God intentionally diminished His light to a lesser degree of power, commensurate with the limited absorbing capacities of the created worlds and beings. Put differently, He rendered His light visible, or revealed it, by limiting it. Thus, while from God's standpoint the zimzum was a withdrawal of divine light, from man's it was a revelation, or flowing out (not in), of divine light.

Since the Hasidic explanation of the zimzum did not include the idea of an inherent conflict within the Godhead, there was no basis for a cosmic catastrophe like the one in the Lurian system. As a result, the shevirah was discussed in homely rather than mythic terms—as in the Maggid's parable about a tailor cutting the cloth before making a suit, for instance.[23] The elimination of the shevirah, and the concomitant obliteration of the dualistic element in the early phases of Luria's cosmic history, made it difficult to explain how the scattered divine sparks had come to be trapped in the worldly realm of evil. Some Hasidic teachers simply ignored the question; others adapted pre-Lurian kabbalistic ideas to provide an answer.

In view of the fact that the same approach to the basic concepts of Lurian theology is found in kabbalistic works dating from the seventeenth and eighteenth centuries, long before the advent of Hasidism, it can hardly be claimed that the Hasidic treatment of Luria's ideas was new or revolutionary. Indeed, kabbalistic thinkers had begun to "demythologize" Luria's system soon after his works were first disseminated. In this sense, therefore, Hasidism was simply following an existing trend whose great exponents included such noted thinkers as Rabbi Joseph Ergas and Rabbi Moses Hayim Luzzatto.[24] Nonetheless, it was only due to Hasidism that the reinterpretation of Luria's symbology by post-Lurian kabbalists ever reached the larger Jewish public.

All in all, Hasidism rejected the Lurian myth to a great extent and returned to the older kabbalistic concepts found in the Zohar and in the writings of Rabbi Moses Cordovero (1522–1570). On the other hand, Hasidism retained both a dualistic attitude toward the world and the Lurian mythology of the trapped sparks, fusing them into a complex new system which rested on three pillars: the doctrine of the uplifting of evil thoughts, the doctrine of communion with God, and the doctrine of the Zaddik. It is to these ideas that we must now turn.

VI

As WAS INDICATED earlier, the cosmic myth at the heart of the Lurianic Kabbalah explained how evil had originated and provided an understanding of the process that would lead to its ultimate abolition. According to the Lurian theology, everything that exists, evil included, is enabled to exist by sustenance received from the good divine light embodied in the trapped sparks that fell during the shevirah. Evil will cease to exist if deprived of sustenance, as will be the case when the sparks are all uplifted and there is a complete separation between good and evil, a state that will be brought about by the performance of the Jewish religious commandments and precepts.

Luria's system held, in other words, that evil would ultimately be destroyed, but in making this claim it failed to answer an important question implicit in the cosmic myth. If evil had its origin in the contradictory element or power in the Godhead that had refused to participate in the zimzum, thus precipitating the shevirah, then evil is derived from the Ein Sof, the source of all goodness; in that case, how can it be completely evil? This pregnant question left the road open for the development of a doctrine maintaining that evil is really a *temporary* manifestation of an aspect of the divine light, and that this element will ultimately be reunited with the good elements and transformed, or returned, to its original state of goodness. More simply, evil was to be redeemed rather than destroyed.

While these two views of evil both relied on the myth of the trapped sparks, there was an enormous theological difference between them, and in addition their practical implications were quite different. Hasidism, by and large, accepted the idea that evil could be redeemed, but was unable at first to formulate a coherent doctrine on the subject.[25] The problem can be demonstrated by a saying attributed to the Besht which deals with the question of what to do if an "external thought" intrudes into one's mind while praying. Since the "external thought" (i.e., an evil thought or simply a thought not connected to prayer) is derived from the evil powers, the question reflects the larger issue of the proper attitude toward evil in general.

In dealing with this question the Besht offered two conflicting modes of behavior. The first—the traditional Lurian model—is to drive the evil thought away. This can be done by reciting a special formula—for example, the names of the evil Canaanite peoples as enumerated in the Torah (Deuteronomy 7:1, etc.). In the Lurian sense, the evil thought that is driven away by means of this technique has been abolished, because a separation has been established between good (the prayer) and evil (the intruding thought). The Besht's other alternative urges the person who is praying to focus his mind on the source of the intruding thought or desire during his prayer. By doing so, he can uplift and redeem the evil thought, weakening the evil powers and strengthening the good divine powers.

The first of these techniques, essentially passive and defensive, requires avoidance of evil, simply driving it away and awaiting its eventual destruction. The second technique, which actively attempts to correct and transform evil, is more commendable from the religious standpoint, but it is also more dangerous. An evil element cannot be uprooted and uplifted unless it has first been permitted to get a hold on one's soul. Since a pious, strictly observant, highly moral person does not normally come into such close contact with evil, he can only practice this method by abandoning the idea of avoidance and actively seeking confrontations with sin. Opening oneself to temptation is always dangerous, however, for it means that one may actually be drawn into sin.[26] As a result, while the doctrine of the uplifting of evil seems to have been widely accepted in early Hasidism, it also met with a certain amount of opposition.

The danger posed by the notion of opening oneself to evil and actively confronting it would probably have been apparent in any period of Jewish history. It was especially obvious in the last decades of the eighteenth century, in the aftermath of the Sabbatian debacle, because of its resemblance to the Sabbatian theology of "redemption through sin," which held that the messiah himself had to assume the guise of evil in order to enter the satanic realm and release the trapped sparks.[27] Based upon the same Lurianic principles that grounded the idea of uplifting evil, this doctrine had been formulated by the more radical Sabbatians as a means of justifying their continued belief in Shabbetai Zevi even though he had ended his life as a sinner and apostate. As the whole Sabbatian episode clearly demonstrated—most notably its tragic culmination in the Frankists, who had endorsed the blood libel and converted to Christianity en masse—it could easily lead to religious anarchy, antinomianism, and national betrayal.

In view of the widespread revulsion at what the Sabbatians had made of this concept, any similar doctrine would inevitably have been tainted for many thoughtful Jews, and as a result the acceptance of the idea of uplifting evil was one of the factors that led to the Mitnaggedic condemnation of Hasidism. Nonetheless, there was a vast difference between the Hasidic and Sabbatian approaches to the question. The Sabbatians, or at least the most radical Sabbatians, held that actually committing sins was an important part of the redemption process. The Hasidic doctrine, on the other hand, was limited to evil *thoughts*, and only a very few passages in the whole body of Hasidic literature can be read as even hinting at the need for actual sinful deeds.

Although undoubtedly influenced by Sabbatian ideas, the doctrine of "redemption through sinful thoughts," as an organic outgrowth of fundamental Lurian concepts, would probably have appeared even if there had never been a Sabbatian heresy. Whether Sabbatianism or the internal dynamics of the Lurian theology made the more important contribution to its development, the doctrine provided a solution to a problem confronting Lurianic thinkers as a consequence of the demythologization of the zimzum and the shevirah outlined earlier, namely, the theological meaning and significance of the trapped divine sparks in the lower realm if the shevirah had not resulted from an inherent conflict within the Godhead and thus was not due to a struggle between good and evil.

To put the question differently, the original Lurian formulation held that the evil powers, which had imprisoned the good sparks, were really evil, but would be destroyed when the sparks were uplifted to their original divine place, thus permitting the world to be redeemed. The newer formulation held that the evil powers were actually of divine origin, and thus potentially good, and the world would be redeemed when they were transformed to good by being uplifted to their proper place in the upper world. From the standpoint of the kind of acts required of the believer, as well as the movement from lower to upper realm, the two uplifting processes are not only similar, they are almost identical. This being so, what is the difference, if any, between the evil powers and the trapped sparks? The early Hasidic teachers did not discuss this question systematically, fusing the two doctrines so completely that there often seems to be no clear distinction between the notions of uplifting the sparks and uplifting evil thoughts and desires. Because of the coexistence of these two doctrines in Hasidic theology, the Hasidic conception of the tikkun became something quite different from the original Lurian tikkun, though its ultimate purpose was the same.

Since the Hasidic theory of the tikkun, based at least in part on the idea of uplifting evil, required direct confrontation with sin, or sinful thoughts, for otherwise evil could not be corrected and uplifted, it still had to deal with the threat posed by the necessity of coming into close contact with evil. The doctrine of the Zaddik, which will be discussed more fully in another section, provided the solution. This doctrine made a distinction between the ordinary Hasid, or simple person, and the Zaddik, a person of superhuman religious abilities. While the Hasid cannot and should not engage in such dangerous practices, and instead should adhere to the older Lurian method of avoiding evil, it is the duty of the Zaddik to undertake the fearsome task of redeeming the world by meeting evil head-on so as to overcome and uplift it. Thus, there was a division of labor, as it were, in regard to the tikkun, with the ordinary Hasidim following the cautious traditional path of avoiding evil and the Zaddik assuming the extreme responsibility of abolishing evil by purifying it in his superhuman soul and uplifting it to its divine origin.

VII

THE LURIANIC KABBALAH, with its central focus on matters of national and cosmic import, saw the ultimate redemption of the people of Israel as a primary goal of Jewish religious endeavor. Hasidism shared this messianic concern, but like the pre-Lurian kabbalistic systems placed its chief emphasis on the idea of *individual* salvation.[28] This is shown by the Hasidic understanding of the tikkun, which retained the Lurian idea of mending and correcting the divine world but stressed its salvific significance for the individual believer, and even more by the idea of communion with God *(devekuth)*, which unquestionably was one of Hasidism's most distinctive and important doctrines.[29]

The Hasidic understanding of the tikkun process of uplifting the trapped sparks and transforming evil into good followed from the belief that every human soul has a special relationship or connection with certain specific sparks that are rooted near its own place of origin in the divine world. Since one's individual fate and well-being are closely bound, as it were, to the fate of the sparks with which one has this intimate connection, performing the acts that will uplift them advances one's own salvific interests as well as the interests of the Jewish people as a whole. As a result, participation in the tikkun process, in addition to its redemptive benefits for the entire people of Israel, offered the individual Hasid a personal benefit commensurate with his own role.

In Luria's system, as in the pre-Lurian kabbalistic literature, the tikkun process had generally been symbolized by the idea of bringing about a union, often described in sexual terms, between Tiferet and Shekhinah, the cosmic male and female principles. Hasidism retained this idea, along with its associated imagery and terminology, but combined it with the idea of devekuth, or communion, which had been a central concept in Jewish ethical literature throughout the Middle Ages.

The medieval thinkers had regarded devekuth as a supreme ecstatic state reserved for a tiny spiritual elite, and even for them not to be achieved without God's help. Hasidism, however, made devekuth into a minimal requirement demanded of anyone who hoped to ascend the spiritual ladder, and also viewed it as an ongoing experience attainable by all Hasidim at least while praying and preferably while engaged in other activities as well. This construct of the ordinary Hasid attaining a state of communion with the

Shekhinah through his own efforts, and not just occasionally but on a continuing basis as a regular part of being a Hasid, is an eloquent manifestation of the Hasidic emphasis on the individual and proved to be one of Hasidism's most characteristic and significant contributions.

Achieving and maintaining the connection with the divine world represented by communion called for an intense degree of concentration and intentionality (kavvanah), and as a result the Hasidic demand for devekuth came into conflict with the halakhic demand for Torah study, which also called for intense concentration, albeit intellectual rather than emotional and visionary. The Hasidic teachers paid lip service to study but obviously considered communion more important. The two kinds of concentration were mutually exclusive, and thus communion and study, unlike many other religious commandments, could not take place simultaneously.[30] Since Hasidic doctrine held that the communion state should not be interrupted unless the devotee himself chose to break it off, many Hasidim tended not to study, thereby indicating, perhaps inadvertently, that for Hasidism an untutored enthusiast in a state of devekuth had greater religious standing than a Torah scholar. The Torah scholars, however, were the Jewish community's leadership class, and Torah study had long held pride of place in the traditional hierarchy of religious activities. Thus it is not surprising that the Hasidic emphasis on communion was seen as a threat to the accepted social order, and in due course it became another of the factors contributing to the Mitnaggedic condemnation of Hasidism.

While the importance of the downgrading of Torah study is not to be denied, a more profound influence was exercised by the idea that communion was not an isolated devotional exercise restricted to the synagogue but something that could be an integral part of all aspects of life, however mundane. Everyday activities like eating, walking, doing business, or engaging in social intercourse, it was held, required only a tiny part of one's spiritual powers and thus should not be a pretext for interrupting the state of communion. Furthermore, since there are divine sparks that can be uplifted in every sphere of life, someone who maintains the appropriate frame of mind while doing something of a worldly, secular nature is performing a genuinely religious act. As fully developed, this idea became the concept of *avodah be-gashmiut*, or "physical worship," which held that the power of communion can transform even a purely physical, material, and secular act into an act of worship in the fullest sense.

The Hasidic theory of communion made extensive use of the kabbalistic concepts of *katnut* ("smallness") and *gadlut* ("greatness"). In the Lurian texts, these terms had applied to the divine powers, with gadlut designating the ideal state of total perfection ordained for each power, and katnut designating the lesser state to which most of the powers were temporarily reduced because of the imperfection of the cosmos in the aftermath of the shevirah. In Hasidic usage the same terms were applied to the two degrees of communion that a person can achieve. In the ideal state of gadlut, the soul withdraws from the world and is immersed in the divine glory. Since the imperfection of man and the world makes it impossible to maintain an unbroken state of gadlut, the devotee is sometimes obliged to descend from gadlut to katnut, a state which is less desirable, but offers the possibility of active participation in worldly life. As will be seen in the next section, it was the application of this idea to the Zaddik, who was held to be constantly moving from imperfect communion in katnut to perfect communion in gadlut, that helped make it possible to see him as an intermediary between this world and the Godhead.

VIII

THOUGH THE KABBALISTIC concept of the righteous man who has a special role in the world's existence antedated and advent of Hasidism by several centuries, Rabbi Isaac Luria's system, which dominated kabbalistic thought in the pre-Hasidic era, did not assign a major function to the messiah or to any other prominent figure. As a result, the Hasidic doctrine of the Zaddik can only be understood in the light of the messianic doctrine of the Sabbatian movement, which resulted from the reworking of Luria's system by Nathan of Gaza, the prophet who proclaimed Shabbetai Zevi as messiah in the year 1665–1666 and formulated the early theology of Sabbatianism.[31]

Luria's conceptualization of the tikkun process had placed the ultimate responsibility for the fate of the divine world, the cosmos, and the people of Israel on the shoulders of the individual Jew. According to Luria, the tikkun would be completed and redemption achieved as a result of a vast collective effort compounded of the ongoing daily activities of all the members of the Jewish people. The messiah would come at the conclusion of the tikkun, but his coming would not be the cause of the redemption, but its outcome—the external sign that the sparks had been uplifted and evil destroyed. Thus, Luria's system had no use for a supernatural leader or, for that matter, for a leader of any kind, and it is significant in this respect that neither Luria nor any of his disciples, even including Rabbi Hayim Vital, who believed himself to have a messianic soul, ever tried to create an institutionalized leadership.

The Lurianic approach was well suited to the daring religious spirit of the elite Jewish community of sixteenth-century Safed, the world center of kabbalistic speculation where Luria and his immediate disciples lived, but it presented far too heavy a burden of responsibility for the great mass of Jews who were neither full-time kabbalists nor religious virtuosos capable of performing prodigious salvific feats. Since charging ordinary people with a role in the tikkun that they could not perform was not only frustrating but made the hope of redemption even more distant, it soon became evident that a redistribution of the theological burden was needed, and this was first provided by Nathan of Gaza, who did so by introducing the idea that the messiah would in fact have a role in the redemptive task, completing the tikkun by performing its final and most decisive phase.

In Nathan's system, the mass of Jews were expected to uplift most of the sparks that were trapped in the lower world, and so were still responsible for effecting a major part of the tikkun. But the phase of the process that was beyond their ability—the uplifting of the sparks that were imprisoned in the deepest stratum of the evil realm—was reserved for the messiah, who would complete the tikkun by the superhuman feat of overcoming evil's darkest powers. Since the messiah would draw the power to perform this task from the faith of those who believed in him, even this final phase of the tikkun was dependent upon an effort by ordinary Jews, but the collective contribution at this point in the process was indirect, a means of infusing the messiah with power, and thus the messiah served, in effect, as a kind of intermediary or agent for the Jewish people as a whole.

While Nathan of Gaza had Shabbetai Zevi in mind when he formulated this idea, which for obvious reasons became an important element of the Sabbatian theology, it had independent standing quite apart from its applicability to the Sabbatian messianic claims. As demonstrated by its acceptance and adaptation by many subsequent Jewish thinkers who had no connection whatsoever with the Sabbatian movement, among them the teachers of Hasidism, there was no need to accept Shabbetai Zevi as the messiah in order to believe, more or less as proposed by Nathan, that the true messiah, whoever he might be and whenever he might come, would play a major role in the process of tikkun and redemption by undertaking the heaviest part of the enormous burden that Luria's system had assigned to the ordinary believer. Indeed, since a compromise along these lines was clearly becoming a historical and theological necessity by the mid-seventeenth century, one may well suspect that an idea of this kind was inevitable, and thus that its connection with Sabbatianism was simply an accident of history.

In any case, the Hasidic doctrine of the Zaddik, at least in its mature form as expounded by the disciples of the Maggid of Mezherich in the last decade of the eighteenth century, was as far from Nathan of Gaza's messianic doctrine as was Nathan's doctrine from the original Lurian system. For Nathan there was one messiah who would perform a magnificent final tikkun, whereas Hasidism envisioned a group of specially endowed individuals, the righteous of every generation, who had to perform tikkunim every day, in every place, whenever the task became too difficult for ordinary pious Jews, the Hasidim. Moreover, the task to be performed by the Zaddik, in comparison with the messiah's task, was partially dependent upon context rather than fixed, and would be defined by the needs and constraints of his own communal and personal situation.

Hasidism, it might be said, fragmented the superhuman messianic hero of Sabbatianism and distributed the pieces across time and space into every generation and every community. This fragmentation, however, did not alter the basic idea, previously absent from Judaism although it flourished in Christianity, of an intermediary role in the redemptive process. The idea was elaborated in Hasidic thought through use of the rich vein of symbolic materials provided by the Kabbalah, especially the symbolism pertaining to the ninth sefirah, variously termed Yesod or Zaddik, whose function it was to serve as an intermediary between the divine and material worlds. Even sexual symbolism was utilized to describe this relationship.

The Hasidic doctrine of the Zaddik evolved in several stages in the period between the Besht and its classic expression by Rabbi

Elimelech of Lyzhansk (1717–1787), taking some of its elements from the pre-Hasidic Kabbalah and others from non-Hasidic sources.[32] While an institutionalized "Zaddikism," developed most fully by the disciples of the Great Maggid, did not exist in the earliest stages, and in addition there were differences of detail and emphasis in various branches of the Hasidic movement—Rabbi Nahman of Bratslav, for instance, maintaining that there could only be one true Zaddik in each generation[33]—the doctrine's main outlines are quite clear and gained general acceptance.

The Zaddik, it was held, possessed unusual spiritual endowments and the ability to ascend to the uppermost divine worlds. Standing in a special relationship to his followers, the Hasidic community with which he was associated, he derived spiritual power from their belief in him and transformed this power into a means of providing them with divine sustenance and protection from the forces of evil. In a more worldly sphere, the people of the community furnished the Zaddik's material support; and the Zaddik, by his spiritual efforts, provided them with the blessings of sons, long life, and sustenance (*baney, hayey, mezoney*). As the instrument through which the community was enabled to touch the divine world and to receive light and sustenance, the Zaddik could not remain in the uppermost realm in a permanent state of supreme communion with God but had periodically to break off, immersing himself in the worldly for a time and then renewing his communion—moving up and down, as it were, in an ongoing process of ascent to gadlut and descent to katnut that was reflected in his moods and exemplified the dynamic character of his spiritual life.

Several aspects of the Hasidic adaptation of ther Lurian theology are manifested in this doctrine. It will be recalled that each human soul was held to have a special relationship or connection with the trapped sparks whose root in the divine world was proximal to its own divine source. Since the Zaddik was responsible for working out the most difficult tikkunim, he was especially concerned with matters pertaining to the sparks with which the members of his community had this kind of relationship. As for the polarity between redeeming evil and separating oneself from it, the Zaddik was expected to confront and uplift sinful thoughts and desires which the ordinary Hasid, effecting the traditional Lurianic separation, could only reject.

This leads to an intriguing question. If the Zaddik was completely pious and spiritually superior, where did the sins he uplifted come from? The answer, which presupposes an intense emotional and psychological relationship between the Zaddik and his followers, held that the sins of the members of the Zaddik's community were transferred to the Zaddik as sinful thoughts. The ordinary Hasid's actual sin or evil desire became a sinful thought in the mind of the Zaddik. By uplifting this thought and re-transforming the evil it embodied to original good, the Zaddik mitigated the Hasid's actual sin; and if the Hasid repented, his repentance would be accepted because of the Zaddik's spiritual efforts. This extremely potent relationship, in which the ordinary Hasid was religiously dependent upon the Zaddik's spiritual power, was given institutional expression in the social organization of the various Hasidic courts and communities.

IX

THE SECULARIZATION OF the Jewish people in the twentieth century has given rise to a nostalgic literature in which Hasidism, as a major spiritual force in the region that was the heartland of traditional Judaism until the Holocaust, has come to assume a central position. Quite understandably, however, modern literary presentations of Hasidism tend to be inaccurate and unhistorical, often crediting it with having originated ethical and spiritual ideas—such as pietism, charity, love for the people of Israel, and benevolent concern for the ignorant and the poor—that have always been an essential part of Jewish religious life, and in some instances treating it as if it were the totality, rather than a distinct branch or movement, of the traditional Judaism of Eastern Europe.

The erroneous belief that Hasidism remains the sole, or primary, spiritual expression of East European Jewry—or, put differently, that Hasidism alone is the authentic Judaism of the era preceding the Holocaust—not only misrepresents the religious life of our East European ancestors but obscures the real contribution of Hasidism to Jewish religious thought and practice. By overemphasizing Hasidic precepts and practices that were typical of Judaism as a whole, it also veils, to an extent, the one basic doctrine that really distinguishes adherents of Hasidism from all other Jews—that is, the belief in the intermediary role of the Zaddik in everyday religious life.

The place of the Zaddik in Hasidism is so important that the very term "Hasid" is incomplete unless joined to the name of a rabbinical dynasty founded by a Zaddik and (with the exception of the Bratslav sect) headed ever since by a line of Zaddikim who are his successors. There is no such things as an "unaffiliated" or "undifferentiated" Hasid except in the minds of those who are insufficiently acquainted with Hasidic life. The Hasidim themselves rarely use the term without a qualifier, identifying one another, for instance, as Bratslav Hasidim, Habad Hasidim, Gur Hasidim, Satmar Hasidim, Vishnitz Hasidim, and so on. Moreover, it is not possible to participate in the religious life of Hasidism without first applying to a particular Hasidic court and deciding to believe in a particular Hasidic rabbi—without deciding, that is, whether one wants to be a Hasid of Rabbi A, of Rabbi B, and so on. This central role of the Zaddik, which might well be called a defining role, is the most important feature of authentic Hasidic religious life. Without minimizing their importance, all the other elements of Hasidism take second place, and it is quite usual to find disagreement over them among the different Hasidic courts.

The misconceptions resulting from the failure to recognize the centrality of the Zaddik are demonstrated by the widely accepted myth that the "simple faith" preferred and cultivated by Hasidism amounts to nothing more than the uncomplicated piety of the ignorant and the unlettered. A faith built upon the exceedingly complex theological idea of an intermediary who serves to connect man and the divine can hardly be called simple.

While it is true that the Zaddik can free an ordinary pious Jew from the obligation of complying with the more difficult requirements of the Lurianic theology, and while it is also true that Hasidism considerably simplified the abstruse Lurian system of intentionality and *yihudim* (prayers and actions designed to bring unity to the divine world), this was a simplification applied to matters that had not been obligatory before the advent of Hasidism and which are not obligatory today outside of Hasidism. In other words, while Hasidism certainly simplified the complex and difficult, its simplifications applied to a higher plane of religious commitment and obligation than was demanded in the other branches of Judaism. The ordinary Hasid may not have been expected to attain the same spiritual level as the Zaddik, and thus it can be said that the role assigned him was "simplified," but nonetheless his role required far more understanding and involvement in processes of ultimately cosmic significance than had previously been expected of those who were not members of a tiny and peculiarly gifted spiritual elite.

In ordinary Hasidic usage, "simple" faith means adherence to the Zaddik and, through him, to God, as opposed to a direct relationship between the individual and the deity. In addition, especially in the terminology of the Braslav sect, "simple" faith often means a faith that is not dependent upon rational considerations and a philosophical foundation—a faith, that is, which derives from acceptance of received tradition rather than scholarly, scientific, or philosophical inquiry. This sense of the term developed early in the nineteenth century when Hasidism came up against the Haskalah, or Jewish Enlightenment movement, and it is reflected in a considerable number of homiletical discussions of the conflict between faith and reason. Thus, the "simple" faith of Hasidism also means a faith grounded in Jewish tradition rather than secular knowledge and deductive reasoning.

From this meaning of "simple" faith we are led to still another sense in which the popular view of Hasidic simplicity is based upon a misconception. A faith grounded in a tradition cannot survive unless its adherents steadfastly study and master that tradition. Thus, it is an outright falsification of fact to maintain, as do many latter-day critics, that Hasidism is "anti-intellectual" or even "non-intellectual." Scholarship in all areas of Jewish religious culture is as fundamental a requirement in Hasidism as in other Jewish denominations, more so than in some. This means serious study of the Torah and the Halakhah as well as scholarly understanding of Jewish theology, especially the Kabbalah, and an intimate familiarity with Judaism's extensive ethical literature, including the writings of Rabbi Moses Hayim Luzzatto, Rabbi Elijah de Vidas, Rabbi Moses Alshekh, Rabbi Isaiah Ha-Levi Horowitz, and other ethical writers of the sixteenth, seventeenth, and eighteenth centuries.

In seeking to understand Hasidism, it is necessary to go beyond superficial impressions. The outer manifestations of Hasidism are often delightfully colorful and "folkish," but they have a deeper meaning. Joyousness, dancing, and music may be essential elements of Hasidic synagogue worship, but in themselves they are not the movement's fundamental doctrines. Sadness and sorrow help the evil powers, while happiness and joy drive them away. The essential idea is the ongoing battle to redeem and uplift the trapped sparks—to transform evil into good and to help the Zaddik in his struggle against the satanic forces. Joy and dancing are simply expressions—not universally accepted in all branches of Hasidism and not practiced by all Hasidim in the same way—of this basic struggle. As this example demonstrates, the religious life of Hasidism can only be understood through its underlying theological meaning, and this entails an understanding of the Hasidic version of the Lurian theological system.

X

THE MODERN STUDY of Hasidism has led to the revision or abandonment of many hoary preconceptions about Hasidic history and theology. One recent example will be presented here because of its importance for an accurate understanding of the Hasidic movement in its early period.

The anti-Hasidic polemical literature circulated by the Mitnaggedim included a document known as the Notes of Rabbi Leib Melamed of Brody. These notes, which caused intense outrage on both sides of the Hasidic-Mitnaggedic conflict, had been found in 1787 in a copy of the *Arba'ah Turim* halakhic code owned by Leib Melamed. Their content was really quite outrageous, revealing the author to have been an antinomian religious anarchist who ridiculed Jewish law and suggested that sexual visions and practices should be an essential part of worship and prayer.

Who was Leib Melamed? The Mitnaggedim claimed he was a Hasid. The Hasidim denied any knowledge of him, maintaining that the notes were a deliberate forgery. Subsequent scholars debated the authenticity of the text and proposed, among other possibilities, that Leib Melamed was a Sabbatian, probably a Frankist, who had wormed his way into a Hasidic community. None of these answers was completely satisfactory though, for the notes seemed to be genuine but showed no trace of specifically Sabbatian or Hasidic ideas.

A possible answer to the riddle was recently offered in a detailed study by Mendel Pierkarz.[34] Analyzing non-Hasidic ethical works written in Eastern Europe in the era before Hasidism and during the movement's early period, Pierkarz surprisingly uncovered a body of theological writings that were clearly not Sabbatian but contained ideas very similar to those in Rabbi Leib Melamed's notes.

It had long been thought that there were only three schools, or trends, in the East European Judaism of the second half of the eighteenth century—Sabbatianism, Hasidism, and Mitnaggedism—but Pierkarz's study of these and other works conclusively demonstrated the existence of a fourth group. The thinkers of this group formulated a radical theology that included some of the same ideas that are an integral part of the Hasidic doctrine of the Zaddik, proving that Hasidism was not so unique in its historical setting as had previously been imagined. They also developed the concept of the uplifting of evil in an especially bold manner. Unlike the Hasidim, however, they did not stop at the threshold of sin and were not satisfied simply to uplift the sinful thoughts and desires that might occur in the normal course of events; instead they advocated the deliberate evocation of sinful thoughts and desires, and perhaps even the committing of actual sins.

The discovery of this previously unknown group shows that social and religious realities in the troubled period when Hasidism originated were even more diverse and complex than once thought. Indeed, the theology, religious symbolism, and possibly even the practices of the fourth group revealed by Pierkarz were much more of a departure from accepted Mitnaggedic norms than the ideas and practices of Hasidism. Still, the group's adherents lived and worked in the midst of Mitnaggedic society without arousing any of the ire that was the lot of the Hasidim for much milder "deviations." The Mitnaggedic rabbis were apparently so preoccupied by the effort to suppress Hasidism that they either ignored or never even noticed the radical thinkers uncovered by Pierkarz.

Since the Mitnaggedim focused their attention solely on the Hasidim, and not on individuals who would seem to have been more natural targets of their wrath, their condemnation of Hasidism must have been motivated chiefly by the movement's social and institutional activities, such as its enmity toward Torah study and talmudic scholars and its creation of a rival leadership establishment in the Zaddikim, and not by its purely religious ideas. Looking at the controversy from the vantage point of two hundred years, with all the benefits of hindsight, one can conclude that most of the Mitnaggedic charges against Hasidism were unfounded. On the other hand, Mitnaggedic opposition, and a desire to prove the Mitnaggedic criticisms unwarranted, may well have prevented Hasidism from straying onto dangerous paths that it might otherwise have explored.

Toward the end of the nineteenth century, as Hasidim and

Mitnaggedim were drawn together by their common opposition to the Haskalah and then to Zionism, the enmity between the two camps began to diminish. The catastrophe that effectively obliterated East European Jewry during World War II transformed what had once been a fierce struggle into a subject for historians.

In our day the time is finally ripe for a dispassionate critical-historical study of the conflict between the Hasidim and the Mitnaggedim, drawing upon the classical texts of the period in an attempt to reveal the genuine spiritual insights and values they embody, rather than imaginary visions conjured up by nostalgia and nightmare.

Notes

[1] See J. Dan, *Ethical and Homiletical Literature* (Hebrew) (Jerusalem, 1975), pp. 3–26, 202–229, 264–272.

[2] *Hebrew Encyclopedia*, vol. 17, pp. 789–795.

[3] Now available in an English translation. D. Ben-Amos and J. R. Mintz, *In Praise of the Baal Shem Tov* (Bloomington: Indiana University Press, 1970).

[4] A detailed exposition of the history of this genre is found in J. Dan, *The Hasidic Story* (Hebrew) (Jerusalem, 1975).

[5] A detailed discussion of the social background of the Hasidic teachers of the first generation is in J. Weiss, "The Early Growth of the Hasidic Way" (Hebrew) *Zion* 16 (1951): 46–105.

[6] Ha-Ari literally means "The Lion," but it is also an acronymn for "The divine Rabbi Yitzhak."

[7] Both J. Weiss and R. Shatz-Uffenheimer have written detailed studies of the Maggid's Mysticism. See especially Weiss, "Via Passiva in Early Hasidism," *Journal of Jewish Studies* 9 (1960); and Shatz-Uffenheimer, *Quietistic Elements in Eighteenth-Century Hasidic Thought* (Hebrew) (Jerusalem: Magnes Press, 1968).

[8] Literally "No End," but this appellation does not have much meaning. Since the infinite Godhead cannot be described in any positive way, even symbolically, any negative term would do equally well—"no beginning," for instance. Ein Sof became the conventional term in Spanish Kabbalah.

[9] The term sefirot is derived from the *Sefer Yetzirah* ("The Book of Creation"), an ancient cosmological work of nonkabbalistic provenance, where it denoted the basic ten numbers that are part of the cosmos and not of the Godhead. It should not be confused with the Aristotelian concept of the spheres (Hebrew: *galgalim*).

[10] The sefirotic system cannot be discussed here in any detail. For a systematic summary of the concept as outlined in the Zohar, see Gershom Scholem, *Major*

Trends in Jewish Mysticism (New York, 1954), especially chap. 6, pp. 205–243.

[11]This basic problem of Lurianic Kabbalah, as well as others discussed here, was treated by I. Tishby in his *The Doctrine of Evil and the Kelippah in Lurianic Kabbalism* (Hebrew) (Jerusalem, 1942). The whole problem is presented in detail in the seventh chapter of Scholem's *Major Trends in Jewish Mysticism*, pp. 244–286.

[12] On dualism in the Zohar, see I. Tishby, *The Teaching of the Zohar* (Hebrew) (Jerusalem, 1949), vol. 1, pp. 285–298. See also G. Scholem, *Von der mystischen Gestalt der Gottheit* (Zurich, 1962), pp. 49–82.

[13] On the later stages of the Sabbatian movement, see G. Scholem, "Redemption Through Sin," in *The Messianic Idea in Judaism* (New York, 1971), pp. 78–141.

[14] A discussion of this class and its social functions will be found in the study of early Hasidism by J. Weiss (cited above, note 1).

[15]The material pertaining to this controversy has been collected and thoroughly analyzed by M. Wilensky, *Hasidism and Mitnaggedim* (Hebrew) (Jerusalem, 1970), vols. 1, 2.

[16]D. Ben-Amos and J.R. Mintz, *In Praise of the Baal Shem Tov*, pp. 55, 57–58; J. Dan, *The Hasidic Story*, pp. 118–122.

[17]I. Tishby, *Paths of Faith and Heresy* (Hebrew) (Ramat Gan, 1964), pp. 204–226.

[18] A. Ya'ari, *Ta'alumat Sefer* (Jerusalem, 1954), pp. 119–142; G. Scholem, in *Behinot* 8 (1955): 79–95; Tishby, *Paths of Faith and Heresy*, pp. 108–168.

[19]D. Ben-Amos and J.R. Mintz, *In Praise of the Baal Shem Tov*, pp. 13–18; G. Scholem, in *Zion* 6 (1941): 89–93; H. Shmeruk, in *Zion* 28 (1963): 86–105; J. Dan, *The Hasidic Story*, pp. 81–83.

[20] This element is hardly mentioned in the stories about the Besht assembled in *In Praise of the Baal Shem Tov*, although it was published in 1815.

[21] A. Shohet, in *Zion* 16 (1951): 30–44.

[22]The famous story about the shepherd's prayer is found in Hebrew and European literature as far back as the twelfth century. See J. Dan, *The Hebrew Story in the Middle Ages* (Hebrew) (Jerusalem, 1974), pp. 179–180 and the bibliography cited there. The "Hasidic" version of the story dates from very late in the nineteenth century.

[23]I. Tishby, in *Hebrew Encyclopedia*, vol. 17, pp. 772–773.

[24] Tishby, *Paths of Faith and Heresy*, pp. 27–29.

[25] For a detailed exposition of this problem, see Tishby, in *Hebrew Encyclopedia*, vol. 17, pp. 784–800.

[26] For a narrative example of this process, see D. Ben-Amos and J. R. Mintz, *In Praise of the Baal Shem Tov*, pp. 86–87. According to this story, Shabbetai Zevi's soul asked the Besht to uplift it, and the Besht agreed. When contact was established between the two souls, however, Shabbetai Zevi tried to drag the Besht down to his own place in hell. The Besht managed to break the contact at the last moment and thus escaped.

[27] G. Scholem, *The Messianic Idea in Judaism*.

[28] The leading scholars today disagree about the extent of the messianic element in Hasidism. B. Z. Dinur, in *Between Generations* (Hebrew) (Jerusalem, 1955), treated messianism as the major driving force in Hasidism, while S. Dubnow, *History of Hasidism* (Hebrew) (Tel Aviv, 1960), pp. 60–63, tended to minimize it.

G. Scholem, in *Major Trends in Jewish Mysticism*, pp. 329–330, and *The Messianic Idea in Judaism*, pp. 176–202, held that Hasidism neutralized the messianic element that had been so strong in Lurianism and Sabbatianism. This view is also held by R. Shatz-Uffenheimer, in *Hasidism as Mysticism* (Hebrew) (Jerusalem, (1968), pp. 168–177. I. Tishby tends to emphasize the messianic element in many Hasidic works but agrees that it is absent in others; see *Zion* 32 (1967): 1–45.

[29] G. Scholem has treated this concept in detail in a paper now included in *The Messianic Idea in Judaism*, pp. 203–226.

[30] See the treatment of this problem by J. Weiss in *Tiferet Yisrael: Rabbi Israel Brody Jubilee Volume* (London, 1967), pp. 151–169; also R. Shatz-Uffenheimer, *Hasidism as Mysticism*, pp. 157–167.

[31] The history of the Sabbatian messianic doctrine has been treated at length by G. Scholem in "Der Berechte," in *Von der mystischen Gestalt der Gottheit* (Zurich, 1962), pp. 83–133.

[32] On the development of the Zaddik doctrine, see, in addition to the paper by Scholem mentioned in note 31, J. Weiss, in *Zion* 16 (1951): 46–105; G. Nigal, *Leader and Congregation* (Hebrew) (Jerusalem, 1962) and *Doctrines of the Author of Ha-Toledot* (Hebrew) (Jerusalem, 1976); R. Shatz-Uffenheimer, in *Molad* 144–145 (1960): 379–390, and *Hasidism as Mysticism*; S. H. Dresner, *The Zaddik* (New York, 1960).

[33] On Rabbi Nahman see J. Weiss, *Studies in Braslav Hasidism* (Hebrew) (Jerusalem, 1975); M. Pierkarz, *Braslav Hasidism* (Hebrew) (Jerusalem, 1972); J. Dan, *The Hasidic Story* (Jerusalem, 1975), pp. 132–187.

[34] M. Pierkarz, *The Development of Hasidism* (Hebrew) (Jerusalem, 1979).

PART ONE

GOD, MAN, AND ISRAEL

THE CREATION

"In the beginning God created" (Genesis 1:1). Understand that the Ein Sof is eternal.[1] It existed long before anything else, and it is the source of everything that has ever come into being, from the depths of the earth to the heights of the highest heaven. One might imagine that whatever exists is eternal, reasoning that all things were hidden within the Ein Sof and integrated with it, but this is not so, because everything else was created. If all other existents are not part of the Ein Sof, however, where did they come from, and what are they made of?

The answer to this is very profound. In the beginning, the original will of the Ein Sof emanated a power from which the world would be made and all the worlds would be separated—the worlds of love, fear, glory, faith, connection, and kingship.[2] Later on, after this power had been emanated, Ein Sof brought into existence that which was potentially within the power, so that things could be revealed and all the worlds could be revealed. Thus, the first emanated power is inextricably bound to the Ein Sof.

(Source: *Kedushat Levi, Likutim: Bereshit*)

1. Ein Sof is the usual kabbalistic designation for the hidden divinity who is beyond even symbolic description.

2. These are symbols of the six lower sefirot—Hesed, Din, Tiferet, Nezah, Yesod, Malchut.

GOD AND SATAN

"And unto thee is its desire, but thou mayest rule over it" (Genesis 4:7). This reminds me of a parable about a king who ruled several provinces, some near and some far away. The king wanted to find out whether the citizens were truly loyal to him, so he disguised one of his servants as a foreign invader and sent him through the kingdom. Some of the people fought against the servant; others offered no resistance. Finally the servant came to a province where there were great scholars. After considering the matter carefully, the scholars asked how the situation could really be as it seemed. There were too many factors that seemed unlikely or impossible. They concluded that the supposed invader had been sent by the king to find out whether the people were loyal. When they told this to the servant, he was very pleased by their wisdom and continued on his way.

The meaning of this parable is clear. It is the same as what Zohar says about the Evil Desire—that it is like a prostitute sent by the king to seduce his son.[1] There is also a deeper meaning, which I heard from my teacher, the Besht. It was the king who disguised himself and came to seduce the queen, etc.—the wise will understand.[2] This principle taught me by my teacher is very important: if you observe very carefully, you will discover that God, blessed be He, is present in every sorrow and misfortune, whether physical or spiritual. The sorrow is God's disguise. Once you realize this, the disguise will be removed and all the sorrows and misfortunes will end.

(Source: *Toledot Ya'akov Yosef: Va'Yakhel*)

1. Zohar II 163b. The Zohar explains that evil is God's means of testing his most faithful worshippers. Satan, therefore, is God's messenger. This approach resolves the question of the autonomy of the evil powers.

2. God disguises Himself as an evil power to tempt the righteous. Compare this with "Satan, Israel, and The Exile," below, pp. 62-64.

GOD'S PRESENCE IN THE WORLD

"May the glory of the Lord endure forever" (Psalms 104:31). Since nothing can withstand God's great light, God concentrates or withdraws Himself through the process of zimzum. A question arises, however, because it might seem more in keeping with the honor due God if the worlds were unable to withstand Him, and it is to answer this that the verse continues: "Let the Lord rejoice in His works." In other words, God wants to rejoice with His works.

To understand this, imagine a father whose child asks for a stick to play with. The child wants to pretend that the stick is a horse. In real life a horse carries its rider, but in this case the rider will have to carry the horse. Since the boy will enjoy playing with the stick, and the father wants his son to be happy, he gives it to him.[1]

The same idea applies to the Zaddikim. They want to lead the world. God wanted them to be happy, so He created the world for them to lead. Since we cannot comprehend the glory of God's inner self but can comprehend the glory immanent in the worlds He created, God concentrated Himself in the worlds. By this means He can enjoy the enjoyment of the Zaddikim who enjoy the worlds.

(Source: *Maggid Devarav Le-Ya'akov*, chap. 7)

1. The parable is very strange. It apparently means that the worlds (i.e., the horse) lead themselves by the power of the immanent God within them, so that the Zaddikim only imagine that they are the leaders.

WISDOM, UNDERSTANDING, KNOWLEDGE

Wisdom, Understanding, and Knowledge[1] exist in everything.

You can understand this by imagining someone who wants to build himself a house. He begins with the idea of a house, *wisdom*, a general thought, and this is symbolized by the letter *yod*, which is nothing but a formless point—a golem, so to speak, substance without form: in other words, the idea of building a house.

Next, using his *understanding*, the man expands and develops his thought. The house will be built according to a certain design, with certain features and "dimensions," and so forth—and all of these concepts are derived from the idea of building a house. This is like the letter *he*, which is *dalet* on *yod*,[2] and it is called "understanding of the heart." The original thought, the idea of the house, is like the father, who provides a drop of semen. Just as the semen alone cannot become a child, so an unformed thought alone cannot become a house. Understanding is like the mother, who gives the drop of semen its form, shaping it properly and rejecting the unclean external elements. Understanding thinks out the plan. It makes distinctions. The house must be one way and not another; it must have a certain number of doors, a certain number of windows, a certain length and width, and so on. One building technique is good, another is not. This process is also called "mother," and it is like the letter *he*, which is *dalet* on *yod*. (This parable will enable you to grasp how the idea of Wisdom, Understanding, and Knowledge refers to God and the creation of the world, but right now we cannot digress to explain this more clearly.)

Once the builder has the house fully planned, the next step occurs. He focuses his thoughts on the plan and adheres to it without deviation. This step is called *knowledge*, and the word has the same sense that it does in the verse, "And the man *knew* Eve" (Genesis 4:1), that is to say, "union." In the beginning the builder was not "united" with his plan, for he still had not decided exactly what he wanted to do. Now he has only one thought—there is a "unity" in his mind—his wisdom is united through his understanding and now he has knowledge—the manifestation of wisdom and understanding. Utilizing this knowledge, the man goes on to build his house. Thus we see that knowledge is the culmination of his original thought—its supreme and comprehensive form. A man who is united with knowledge in this way goes on to build the "house" of his mind with further knowledge of the same kind, just as it says in Psalms: "And by knowledge are the chambers filled" (Psalms 24:4).[3]

And the same holds true if you wish to achieve communion with God. God must be Wisdom, Understanding, and Knowledge for you. The wisdom aspect is the tradition, handed down by our fathers and our rabbis, that there is a God in the world—but this alone is a thought without form. Through understanding you then must make distinctions and consider how God observes everything and gives life to all of us—how the worlds are filled with God. By contemplating the things of the world in this way—that is, by deducing an awareness of God's presence through contemplating the world—you begin to understand God's existence. Once this idea is fully and completely formed in your mind, you will always retain this knowledge. While still in the stage of understanding, you may not always focus your thoughts on God—your mind may wander to other things, heaven forbid. But once your mind and thoughts have completely accepted this idea, once it becomes knowledge, then it will always be part of you, united in your mind and dwelling within you forever.

(Source: *Yosher Divrey Emet* by Rabbi Meshulam Feibush, chap. 21)

1. The three higher sefirot in kabbalistic symbolism. Wisdom (Hokhmah) also symbolized as the father, and Understanding (Binah), also symbolized as the mother, both play a major part in the description of the early stages of the creation of the world, before material things were created.

2. The Hebrew letter *he* is described as a *dalet* to which the point of the *yod* has

been added: Usually, in kabbalistic symbolism, Hochmah is the *yod* and Binah is the first *he* in the holy name of God.

3. The parable is derived from the preceding verse: "Through wisdom a house is built, and by understanding it is established" (Proverbs 24:3).

THE PURPOSE OF CREATION

Love and fear of God can only be achieved with the help of the Zaddikim of the generation, because the Zaddik of the generation is the one who reveals love and fear of God.[1]

The Zaddik continually tries to reveal God's wishes. God's will is reflected in everything that exists. This is true of the entire creation taken as a whole, because God wanted to create the whole world, and it is also true of every detail of the creation. There is an element of God's will in everything because God wanted every detail, every single thing, to be exactly as it is, with its own specific shape, nature, capability, pattern of behavior, and so forth.

In order to understand God's will and purpose, the Zaddik constantly searches for these elements of the divine will. He tries to understand, for instance, why God gave the lion a tawny mane and made him powerful and carnivorous, and why He made the flea tiny and weak. He is even interested in less obvious details: why the lion's paw is made one way, his tail another way, his mane still another way. And he is equally interested in everything else in the world, whether animal, mineral, or vegetable, whether human being or brute creature. There are vast differences between the various species, and between the individual members of each species. It is the same with trees and shrubs and every other aspect of the creation. There is a vast diversity of shapes, patterns, powers, natures—and all of this came about because the blessed Creator willed it to be this way.

The Zaddik constantly searches for these elements of the divine will and he understands them in accordance with the glory that he finds in Israel as a whole, because the whole world was created for Israel's sake. This is shown by the verse "In the beginning" (Genesis

1:1) because God was thinking of Israel before the creation and therefore Israel is called the "beginning."[2] Moreover, as shown by the verse "Israel, in whom I will be glorified" (Isaiah 49:3), God was thinking about the glory and love He would receive from Israel in the future.

It is for this reason that God created the world. Thus we find that the whole world was created for the sake of the glorification that Israel would render to God. Just as the totality of the creation was for the sake of the totality of the glory that God would receive from Israel, so the details and particulars of the creation were for the sake of the details and particulars of the glory that God would receive from Israel. Within every Jew there is an individual detail, or aspect, which glorifies God. This is true of the lowliest person; it is even true of sinners, so long as they continue to belong to the people of Israel. Every Jew has his own individual element of glorification by means of which he can glorify God.

This is true, also, of the smallest details. There is a tiny element of glorification in every limb and every act of every Jew, and each element is different from all the others. Thus, God can be glorified even by the slightest movement of a single hair on the head[3] of the most humble member of the entire Jewish people.

By constantly seeking and finding these many tiny and particular aspects of the glorification that is within every member of the people of Israel, the Zaddik comes to know and understand God's will as reflected in the creation of the world, both in general and in particular. This is because God's will in the creation as a whole was directed toward His glorification by Israel, and every single thing in the creation was created by virtue of that overall will. Every single thing was given powers, characteristics, and a nature in accord with that will, which is equivalent to the glorification within every member of the people of Israel.

As a result, when the Zaddik comes to understand the glorification in Israel, both in general and in every particular aspect, he understands all of the divine will that is embodied in the creation as a whole and in particulars of the creation, down to the tiniest detail.

(Source: *Likutey Moharan* I, chap. 17)

1. In this sentence Rabbi Nahman uses the phrase "Zaddik of the generation" in both the singular and the plural. This reflects the view that every generation has but one true Zaddik, though there were many Zaddikim throughout history.

2. Compare Bereshit Raba, chap. 1; Va-Yikra Raba, chap. 36.

3. Literally *peah*, the lock of hair beside the ear that Orthodox Jews leave uncut. Rabbi Nahman used this expression to give a religious meaning to "slightest movement."

THE IMMANENT GOD

Every Jew is a part of God above. The heart is the seat of this divine immanence. Since the divine power in the Jew's heart derives from the Ein Sof, whose light and brilliance are infinite, there is no end to the Jew's desire for God. This passionate desire for God, by its very limitlessness, could prevent the Jew from doing anything and thus make it impossible for him to implement his good qualities.

The situation was the same at the beginning of the creation. Since everything was Ein Sof, there was no space to create in. God wanted His kingdom to be revealed, however, and this could only be achieved by means of the various qualities, or worlds, through which we can grasp the ideas of His divinity and spread the knowledge that there is a master and ruler and leader over all. So God contracted the light of Ein Sof and created the worlds in the empty space that remained.

Similarly, we each must contract the infinite light and brilliance in our hearts so as to be able to worship God in small stages and in a measured way. God wants our worship to be encompassed in good qualities, for through these qualities His kingdom is revealed.

(Source: *Kitzur Likutey Moharan* 49a)

SUPREME KNOWLEDGE

Only God, who lives forever, has eternal life, but since God is the source, whoever achieves union with God will also live forever. If you become part of the true Unity, achieving oneness with God, you will live eternally like God.

Similarly, there is no perfection but the perfection of God; everything else is imperfect, but whoever becomes part of God achieves perfection.

Inclusion in God's oneness is the essential and fundamental requirement.[1] It is achieved through knowledge of God, as is indicated by the proverbial saying, "If I knew him I would have been he." Since the mind is man's most important faculty, whatever the mind is thinking determines where the rest of him is. If someone achieves knowledge and understanding through the divine knowledge, then he actually becomes part of the divine knowledge. The more one knows, the more one becomes an integral part of the source—a part, that is, of the Holy One, may He be blessed.

Lack of knowledge, however, causes poverty, childlessness, sickness, and all other human ills. You may object that some people seem to have everything they want and are quite happy even though they are totally devoid of knowledge. The truth is that they have nothing at all, because without knowledge, whatever they have is nothing. By the same token, while it sometimes seems as if those who have complete knowledge are experiencing deprivation of one kind or another, they actually want for nothing, because the imperfect things they lack add up to nothing. The talmudic sages had this in mind when they said: "If you have acquired knowledge, what do you lack? And if you lack knowledge, what do you have?" (B. Nedarim 41a).

Knowledge is the root of both perfection and imperfection. It is also the root of the evil attributes of anger and cruelty, both of which derive from the absence of knowledge, or from imperfect knowledge. This is shown by the verse that says, "For anger resteth in the bosom of fools" (Ecclesiastes 7:9). It also explains why sick people so often feel angry: during their illness they are controlled by the *dinim*,[2] or evil powers, and *dinim* are mind in its lowest state.[3]

In the future, in the time of the coming redemption, knowledge will be revealed to all mankind, and everyone will know God. As it says in the Bible, "For the earth shall be full of the knowledge of the Lord" (Isaiah 11:9). Once this happens, anger will no longer exist, and that is why the same text also says: "And the wolf shall dwell with the lamb, and the leopard shall lie down with the kid . . . . And the cow and the bear shall feed . . . . They shall not hurt nor destroy. . . .For the earth shall be full of the knowledge of the Lord" (Isaiah 11:6–9). In our time, since anger is still in power, it is impossible for a wolf and a lamb to dwell together, but they will be able to do so in the future, when evil is abolished by the revelation of the power of knowledge.

In the days of the redemption, everyone will know God, even the gentiles, for the earth will be full of the knowledge of the Lord. But in the here and now, we Jews can already know everything that the gentiles will know only in the future. As for the additional knowledge we shall have at that time, it cannot even be discussed now, because our present knowledge is derived from the category of the "surrounding knowledge."[4]

Whatever apparent advantages and perfections the gentiles have now really add up to nothing, because "If you lack knowledge, what do you have?" Furthermore, all gentile achievements and triumphs are really for our benefit. In the future, when the earth is full of knowledge and they know the Lord, the gentiles themselves will understand this, as is shown by the following verse: "Then said they among the nations: The Lord hath done great things with these: the Lord hath done great things with us" (Psalms 126:2). In other words, whatever great things the Lord has done "with these"—the gentiles in the present world—he has really done "for us"—for the benefit and greatness of Israel. In the future, when they have obtained knowledge and understanding, the gentiles will understand this. Since our knowledge will be much greater than theirs, we will find the whole idea ridiculously simple, and that is why the same verse begins with the words: "Then was our mouth filled with laughter. . . .Then they said among the nations: The Lord hath done great things with these" (Psalms 126:2). Our knowledge will be so great that we will regard the gentile level of knowledge as laughable.

All of this explains why life in the future will be eternal. When knowledge is revealed, we will all be included in the Divine Unity. Our blessed sages demonstrated their understanding of this idea in their interpretation of "In that day shall the Lord be one, and His name one" (Zechariah 14:9). In discussing this verse (in B. Pesachim 50a), the sages asked: Isn't God already one? They answered: In the present world we have a blessing to be recited when something unfortunate happens, "Blessed be the true judge," and another to be recited when something good happens, "The good [and] benefactor," but in the future there will be only one blessing for everything, "The good [and] benefactor." In other words, in the future, when knowledge is revealed, it will become clear that nothing in God's world is evil or unfortunate—everything is good, and all is one.

The exile also derives from lack of knowledge, as shown by the verse, "Therefore my people are gone into captivity[5] for lack of knowledge" (Isaiah 5:13), and knowledge will be the source of deliverance, as shown by the verse, "And ye shall *know* that I am the Lord your God who brought you out from under the burdens of the Egyptians" (Exodus 6:7). And for this reason, Moses, who had knowledge,[6] was the agent of the redemption from Egypt.

It is important to remember, however, that even in the future, when the earth is full of knowledge and the Surrounding Mind has become Immanent Mind, there will still be other surrounding powers. This is because God's true essence will not be known to everyone. Each person will understand in accordance with his own spiritual level, his own worship of God, and the amount of trouble and effort with which he has worked and suffered for God in the present world. Everyone, including the gentiles, will be on a higher spiritual level than now, but there will still be a great difference between Jews and gentiles. What the gentiles will regard as profound understanding and a great intellectual achievement will seem simple-minded and laughable to us, hardly true understanding at all. As was stated above, "Then was our mouth filled with laughter and our tongue with singing. Then said they among the nations: The Lord hath done great things with these" (Psalms 126:2). By the standards of the present world, of course, the gentiles really will have attained an understanding of something profound when they finally come to understand the greatness of Israel and realize that all their own achievements and triumphs have only been for Israel's sake. Even so, since our own understanding and knowledge will be so much greater, we will not regard this as understanding at all, but as something simple-minded and silly.

Just as there will still be a difference between Israel and the nations, so there will be differences between individuals within Israel—even between one righteous person[7] and another, not to mention between righteous people and evil people. This is because what surrounds one degree will be immanent to another degree, for in the Common Mind all will be equal and all will know God, even the gentiles, but in the deeper layers of wisdom, each person will achieve in accordance with his own degree. To understand this, imagine the waters in the sea.[8] On the surface, no matter where you look, the water seems the same, but beneath the surface there are many differences: in one place the water is shallow and close to land; in other places it is deeper; in still other places it is virtually bottomless. The same is true of the various degrees of understanding God.

This also explains what the sages meant when they said that every Zaddik will be burned by the canopy of another Zaddik (B. Bava Batra 75a).[9] When a Zaddik attains a totally new degree of understanding, he becomes so impassioned that he burns from the fire of the new knowledge he has acquired. But a Zaddik who has already attained the same degree of understanding and passed beyond it, and now is busy learning something even more profound, does not share this passion. When it is said that every Zaddik is burned and burning and impassioned by the canopy of his friend, it means that each Zaddik is so intensely affected by the knowledge appertaining to the colleague immediately above him that he is "set afire" by it and must cover and protect himself,[10] while the very same degree of knowledge seems elementary to the Zaddik it properly appertains to, and therefore he is not affected in any such manner.

(Source: *Likutey Moharan* I, chap. 21)

1. Hebrew: *iqar ha-kelaliyut*, literally: "the basic element of the totality."

2. *Dinim* here are evil powers, but the word is derived from the idea that God's judgments (*dinim*) are the source of the evil that afflicts man. In later Kabbalah the term is used to describe evil powers in general.

3. *Mohin de-katnut*, divine powers from the "mind" of God; (i.e., the highest sefirot, when they are in a lowly stage, according to the Lurianic Kabbalah). In Hasidism the term is used to describe human "states of mind": when the *mohin* are in a "great" state, a person (usually the Zaddik) is close to God, whereas when they are in a "low" state, the evil powers can have a hold on the Zaddik's soul.

4. Rabbi Nahman expounds his version of this basic kabbalistic concept (*sechel makif*, the surrounding mind, and *sechel penimi*, the immanent mind) in the second half of the homily.

5. Hebrew: *galah*, "went into exile."

6. "Knowledge" as a divine sefirah. The sefirah usually connected with redemption, and especially with the redemption from Egypt, is Binah (literally: "understanding").

7. Hebrew: *zaddik*; it is unclear whether Rabbi Nahman means a righteous person in general or a Zaddik in the Hasidic sense of the word.

8. Rabbi Nahman is referring to Isaiah 11:9: "For the earth shall be full of the knowledge of the Lord, as the waters cover the sea."

9. According to the sages, in the Coming World every Zaddik will have seen canopies of fire, and each Zaddik will be burnt by his neighbor's canopy. See Rashi's comment on this passage.

10. *Lehapot*, "to cover oneself or protect oneself," derived from the same root as *hupa*, "canopy."

MYSTICISM AND KABBALAH

My holy teacher, Rabbi Menahem Mendel,[1] blessed be his memory, taught that the term *nistar*, or "secret," is applied to something that you cannot explain to someone else.[2] For example, since it is impossible to describe adequately the taste of a food to someone who has never eaten it, this is properly called a "secret word." The same is true of the love and fear of God. It is impossible to describe to someone else the feeling of love in your own heart. and thus it is called "secret." How is it possible, then, to say that the teachings of the Kabbalah are secret? After all, the book is right there for anyone who wants to study it; a person who cannot understand what he reads is ignorant, and if that is the kind of person we are talking about, we might just as well say that the Talmud is "secret."

The genuinely secret element in the Zohar and the writings of Rabbi Isaac Luria is that they are based upon communion with God and thus are intended only for those who are able to be watchers of the holy chariot—as was Isaac Luria, of blessed memory, who knew all the paths of heaven and always walked them in his mind, like the four sages who entered the Pardes.[3]

The difference between a person who is constantly contemplating God and one who is not is clarified by imagining someone who briefly meets a stranger from another town and then does not recognize him when they meet again later on. He does not recognize the stranger because when they first met, the stranger's image did not register on his mind and made no impression on his memory. As a result, he cannot "unite" with the stranger when they encounter each other a second time—it is as if they do not know each other. This is exactly what happens to someone who contemplates God only occasionally and when he is "in the mood." He will never come to know God or to love God or to have communion with God.

On the other hand, someone who contemplates God constantly, or at least at every possible opportunity, is like someone who sees another person several times in different ways. The other person's image is imprinted in his heart and remains with him even when the other is far away.

(Source: *Yosher Divrey Emet*, chap. 22)

1. Rabbi Menahem Mendel of Premishlan, a disciple of Rabbi Dov Baer of Mezherich.

2. *Nistar* is frequently used as a designation for the Kabbalah. Following the teachings of Rabbi Menahem Mendel, Rabbi Meshulam is making a distinction between wisdom that is really "secret" and wisdom that can be communicated in words, which is not really "secret." The kabbalistic literature falls into the latter category because it is written and communicated in words, unlike real "secrets," which by definition cannot be communicated by means of human speech or writing. Such an attitude toward the theology of the Kabbalists is relatively unusual in Hasidic literature.

3. See B. Hagigah 14b.

THE UNION OF THE SHEKHINAH

Everyone should pray for the light of the moon to be the same as the light of the sun,[1] and for the moon to be complete, with nothing missing or diminished, for this means that there will no longer be an evil element and all the satanic powers will be destroyed, in fulfillment of the verse which promises: "In that day shall the Lord be one and his name one" (Zechariah 14:9). The meaning of this verse is as follows: the holy name will be composed of the letters *yod he yod he*. There will no longer be a separation between the *vav* and the *he*,[2] like the one between *yod* and *he*, and then the word *meorot* ("lights"), which is now spelled without a *vav*, will be completed by the addition of a *vav*. The *vav* is a symbol of the Tree of Life. It stands for the emanations flowing from the Tree, for all life, blessing, and goodness emanate from the Tree of Life, and the divine emanation received by the Tree flows from the divine light that enlightens it.

If something is missing from the light that flows down to the Tree of Life, it will also be missing from the divine emanation that in turn flows from the tree. The Shekhinah is called "moon" because she has no light of her own, just as the moon receives all its light from the sun. Symbolically, the Shekhinah is like a mirror; she does not have her own source of light, and whatever light she receives from comes from God.

But when the ultimate union of Shekhinah and God takes place, with nothing missing and nothing lacking, all the emanations of goodness and blessing will completely and freely descend—and then all the evil powers, and all the satanic elements, will be destroyed.

(Source: *Degel Mahane Ephraim Tazria*)

1. The moon is the symbol of the Shekhinah, the last sefirah, whereas the sun is the symbol of Tiferet, the sixth sefirah. Tiferet and Shekhinah are husband and wife. God intended them to be of equal luminosity, but because of the imperfection of the created world, the Shekhinah lost most of her light. At the End of Days the equality will be restored.

2. The letter *vav* in the tetragrammaton stands for Tiferet, and the last letter, *he*, stands for Shekhinah. In the description of the creation of the sun and the moon in Genesis 1:14, the word *meorot* ("lights") is spelled without a *vav*. This will be rectified in messianic times.

THE SECRET OF THE CONTRACTION OF THE MOON

"And God made the two great lights: the greater light to rule the day, and the lesser light to rule the night; and the stars" (Genesis 1:26). This verse tells us that God emanated all the worlds and created existence *ex nihilo*. His purpose in doing this was to make it possible for the Zaddik to transform existence into nothingness[1] and to submit all the divine powers to God, for as King David of blessed memory said, "Thine, O Lord, is the greatness and the power" (I Chronicles 29:11).[2] The Zaddik uplifts all the powers to their original source, where they will be sweetened.

. . . God contracted Himself from one stage to the other until four forms, four elements, emerged . . . for God contracted the moon—that is, He went from one contraction to the other until He came to the earthly world, the physical world. This reveals the secret meaning of the contraction of the moon. Before God came to the divine powers there was no difference between rich and poor and there was no "small." Everything had been created in greatness. But when God entered the divine powers, "great" and "small" were created. Why? So that the Zaddik would be able to make nothing out of something and could uplift the physical powers to their source, as we mentioned above . . . and when the Zaddik does this, he brings life to all the worlds.

(Source: *Pri Ha-Aretz: Bereshit*)

1. "Existence" (in Hebrew, *yesh*) is the symbol of the second sefirah, Hochmah (Wisdom), whereas "nothing" (*ayin*) is a symbol of the first and highest, Keter (Crown).

2. This verse, according to kabbalistic homiletical exegesis, contains the names of the seven lower sefirot. Here the author interprets the opening words, "Thine, O Lord," as "To you, O Lord," meaning that the powers enumerated in this verse will be returned to God, from whom they emanated, with the help of the Zaddik.

THE SECRET MEANING OF NOAH

"These are the generations (*toldot*) of Noah. Noah was in his generations a man righteous (*zaddik*) and wholehearted; Noah walked with God" (Genesis 6:9). Why does the text say that Noah was righteous? Because Zaddikim "generate" good works.[1] What good works did Noah generate? He brought peace and wholesomeness into the world by uplifting the divine powers to their source, a place of peace and wholesomeness where there are no evil powers, and there, as they were sweetened within their source, the evil elements fell off and the divine sparks were uplifted. That is why the text says that Noah was "a man righteous and wholehearted"; he connected all the powers to wholesomeness, and then all the powers that were in lowly stations within the evil powers became powers of mercy and were able to receive divine life from the divine powers.

(Source: *Pri Ha-Aretz: Noah*)

1. The homily here is derived from the fact that two Hebrew words in the verse cited have dual meanings. *Zaddik*, usually translated "righteous," as in the biblical quotation, was also the title of the Hasidic rabbis (Zaddikim). *Toldot*, translated "generations" in the quotation, can also mean "results" or "outcomes." Hence: the works, or results, of the Zaddikim are good works.

NOAH AND ABRAHAM

There is a midrashic parable explaining the difference between Noah and Abraham (B. Nedarim 32a). Both of them, it says, are like people who love the king. Noah, however, is a man sitting in the darkness, and he has light only when the king brings it to him. Abraham, on the other hand, brings a light to the king; when he does, the king says: "Don't bring your light here where there is already light; take it to someplace dark."

. . . In other words, Noah was righteous (*zaddik*) in his faith but lacked philosophical understanding. Since his deeds were wholesome, God gave him light. As for Abraham, even at the tender age of three he knew his Creator through study and intellectual investigation. His knowledge increased year by year, and so did his wisdom and understanding. At the same time, though, he remained wholesome in all his deeds—and this means by faith alone, as we know from the verse "Walk before Me, and be thou wholehearted" (Genesis 17:1). God is saying to Abraham: "Walk before Me," meaning above the powers, and then "be wholehearted."

Understanding of God refers to Ein Sof, the supreme Godhead. Communion with the Ein Sof can be achieved only through faith, as is shown by the example of the worlds themselves, which are connected to each other by faith. We see this even in our earthly world. For example, an infant has no understanding, but even so, a father is pleased when his infant child seems to know him. The same applies to the creation of all the worlds, as is shown by the phrase, "In the beginning God created" (Genesis 1:1). Israel, which is called the "beginning," knew how to praise its Creator, calling him "Our Father" and "Our Creator." As is suggested by the talmudic saying that the cow wants to nurse even more than the calf wants to suck (B. Pesachim 112a), this praise is pleasing to God. In fact, it is in the very nature of the connection between each world and the one directly below it that each superior spiritual power wants to provide its emanation to the one directly inferior to it. Indeed, the superior world derives more pleasure from providing the emanation than the inferior one derives from receiving it.

Our parable, however, does not really reflect the true situation. The worlds were all created, and the kind of connection we have been discussing is part of the natural order of creation, but none of this applies to the First Cause, God, the Ein Sof, may He be blessed—the Creator who created everything, including the natural order of creation. Pleasure means nothing to the Creator, and neither does this connection we have been discussing, because He created nature, and He provides for everything and gives existence to everything at every moment. If there were even one tiny instant in which He did not will that everything should exist, everything would instantaneously cease to exist, and it would be as if it had never existed.

In light of this, what possible meaning can be attached to the connection with Him and the emanation coming from Him? As we have mentioned, there is nothing but God's will to create. With His will God created everything in the beginning, and with His will He continues to give existence and to provide emanation, and He receives pleasure—but this is completely beyond human comprehension; there is no way for us to understand it.

. . . The essence of worship and the connection with God is to achieve the true communion which is beyond all speculative understanding. Connection with God is not comprehension of God, for God is outside the creation and beyond all loving, beyond the nature of the connection discussed above. He is the Creator who created everything, and communion with Him can be achieved only by faith.

(Source: *Pri Ha-Aretz: Lech Lecha*)

JERUSALEM THE HEART

"Comfort ye, comfort ye My people, saith your God. Bid Jerusalem take heart, and proclaim unto her that her time of service is accomplished, that her guilt is paid off; that she hath received of the Lord's hand double for all her sins" (Isaiah 40:1–2).

In order to understand "bid Jerusalem take heart," we must understand the connection between heart and Jerusalem. We must also understand the meaning of "She hath received of the Lord's hand double for all her sins," for it seems strange that God would double their punishment, heaven forbid, because of their sins.

All this is made clear by something I learned from my master, my grandfather of blessed memory, the Besht. He taught that the king of Israel is the heart of Israel, and that the heart, which hears and understands, is the king of the body and its limbs. Just as the royal army will not go into action without the king's knowledge, so the limbs behave in accordance with the heart's dictates, for the heart hears and understands, and in it resides the life-force that animates the whole body. Unless the heart so directs, it is not possible for a person to lift an arm or a leg. Moreover, I have read in the *Reshit Hochmah*[1] that the heart is called "Jerusalem," for it is located in the middle of the body, just as Jerusalem is located at the center of the world.

. . . We find, therefore, that the heart was created to be God's residence, but since God does not reside in a heart unless it is broken and humble, a heart can only be regarded as complete when it is broken and humble. When it is complete, it is called "Jerusalem the holy city." When the heart is Jerusalem, her king is the spirit inside her—the broken spirit.

(Source: *Degel Mahane Ephraim: Va'ethanan*)

1. "The Source of Wisdom" by Rabbi Elijah de Vidas of Safed (late sixteenth century), one of the most frequently quoted ethical works in Hasidic literature.

BETWEEN MAN AND ANIMAL

Our blessed sages, noting that the term *reshit* ("beginning") is applied to Israel in the Torah, explained *be-reshit* (Genesis 1:1; usually translated "In the beginning") as meaning that the creation took place "for Israel."[1] In consequence of this, we must all be completely consistent in our work of worshiping the Creator day and night, every hour and every moment, so that we will never lose our special chosen status. Other peoples may pursue their various desires and ambitions, but we, the people of Israel, who claim that God chose us from among the nations and say so in our prayers, should not behave as they do. If we do as the other nations do, performing the same forbidden acts, what difference would there be between us? If we were to do the same things as the other nations, heaven forbid, then what we say in our prayers would be a lie, but an Israelite's worship should be on a higher spiritual level than a gentile's.

In all such matters the rule is as follows. In order to perfect yourself and unite yourself with God and totally accept the yoke of the divine kingship, you must be in a state of constant fear that will prevent you from doing anything that is not for God—whether it be a great deed or a small one, even an earthly thing like eating, drinking, sleeping, or any other worldly pleasure. You must remain constantly aware that everything was created in wisdom by the Creator, and that all things contain hints of the divine wisdom which can help you to achieve the supreme divine light as well as spiritual pleasures far beyond the pleasures deriving from material things.

While the divine pleasures far surpass any earthly pleasures, they have been incorporated in earthly, created things so as to make it possible for you to achieve the highest through the lowly, and so that every human heart can be awakened to the worship of the Creator. If you do not awaken to your Creator, you are nothing more than an animal, seeking only to fulfill your animal desires, and thus the element that makes man superior to the beasts disappears. But if you fulfill all the practical commandments, and do so with communion at some spiritual level, you connect the earthly pleasures to their original source in the divine first thought. And this is the main purpose of all human worship in this world—to uplift the various pleasures to the original united source.

(Source: *Or Ha-Meir: Bereshit*)

1. Compare Jeremiah 2:3, and the homily in *Otiot DeRabbi Akibah* (Wertheimer ed.) 357.

DIVINE JUSTICE

"For they persecute him whom Thou has smitten. . . .Add iniquity unto their iniquity; and let them not come unto Thy righteousness. Let them be blotted out of the book of the living" (Psalms 69:27–29). My teacher the Besht explained this verse to us. He began by asking why they should be punished when the verse means that they did what God ordered them to do, and then he told the following parable.

Once upon a time there was a king of Edom who was a very pious pagan. He invited several other kings and rulers to a banquet, and after the wine had put him in a cheerful mood, he asked his guests to tell him about their gods. They all gave a full account of their beliefs. While all of them preferred their own idols, each admitted that the king's idol had merits of one kind or another.

When the Jews were asked the same question, one of them was very wicked, and this made the king quite sad. So he told the Jew a story. An expert on precious stones, he said, once had a gemstone with a flaw. In order to get rid of it, he disguised himself as a peasant and, pretending to know nothing about precious stones, sold it to someone else. The man he sold it to sold it to another man, and so on, until the stone finally came into the hands of the king. When the king asked his own experts to appraise the stone, they all flattered him by saying that it was very valuable. Finally he asked the expert who had originally sold the stone, and this man told the king that the stone was worthless. The king was furious, but the man said, "Believe me, I know. I was the stone's original owner, and I disguised myself in order to sell it."

It is the same with idolatry. No one knows the true nature of idolatry better than someone who is of the true seed of Israel. This enables us to understand what David said to God in the verse from Psalms quoted above, for God gives suffering to a righteous person only through the medium of a wicked person and not by means of another righteous person.[1]

(Source: *Toledot Ya'akov Yosef: Pinhas*)

1. The Besht was explaining why those whom God commands to punish Israel will themselves be punished—they were chosen for the task because they were already deserving of punishment. Since the parable and the homiletical context are not in complete harmony, it is evident that they are independent of each other.

MAN'S INFLUENCE ON THE DIVINE

"Noah was in his generation a man righteous *(zaddik)* and wholehearted" (Genesis 6:9). Similarly, in every generation there is a Zaddik who is the foundation of the world.[1] Take special note of one thought which will awaken your hearts to perform *yihudim*[2] in the divine world, for this expression refers to eating.[3]

. . . Anything in the world can help to cause *yihudim* in the divine world . . . . If these things cause you to awaken, hinting at the divine wisdom that causes the descent of the divine plenty and awakens your heart to the worship of God, you will be able to bring about an increase in the divine plenty and light, so that there is more than before.

To put it briefly, every Jew has the ability to perform *yihudim* in the divine world in accordance with the power of his knowledge and spiritual achievements, uplifting all the holy letters from all the creatures in the world. All the creatures were created by the holy letters of the Torah and return to the place from whence they came, causing divine light to flow to these stages in the divine world.

This applies only to a wise man who fears God and worships truly with all his might, directing his every effort and all the details of his worship to pleasing God. Such a person can really gather the letters of the Torah from everything in the world, even from a simple conversation with another person. Someone who does not have an expanding mind cannot do this . . . although he can unify himself with the letters of the Torah when he studies or prays.

(Source: *Or-Ha-Meir: Beshalah*)

1. Following Proverbs 10:25: "But the righteous *(zaddik)* is an everlasting foundation." Since the Hebrew *olam*, "everlasting," can also mean "world," the verse can be read: "But the Zaddik is the foundation of the world."

2. See "The Ascension of the Besht's Soul," note 8, below pp. 96–98.

3. The author provides a homiletical explanation of the equation between "eating" and "intercourse" *(yihud)*.

ISRAEL AND THE WORLD

Certain heretics claim that the world exists because it has to exist, and they think they can demonstrate this false idea with proofs derived from the laws of nature. The truth is, however, that the whole idea is utter nonsense. The claim that the world's existence is necessary is totally false. Only God's existence is necessary; everything else is contingent on God's will. Everything that exists was created from nothing by God, and it is in His power to create or not to create; thus the whole world and everything in it is contingent, not necessary.

The mistaken notion[1] that the world's existence is necessary takes its origin from the fact that the world's existence became necessary once the souls of Israel were emanated and derived from the divine powers. As is well known, the whole world and everything in it was created only for the sake of Israel. Once the souls of Israel were emanated and created, therefore, it was as if God had to create and sustain the world, since He had emanated the souls of Israel so that He could create all the worlds for them.

At the time when God emanated the souls of Israel, their existence, and the existence of all the worlds that are dependent on them, was of a contingent nature, since God could either have created them or not created them. Once God became willing to emanate the souls of Israel, the whole world entered into the category of necessary existence; for once the souls of Israel had been emanated, it was as if God were compelled to bring the world into existence, since the purpose of their emanation was so that the worlds would be created for their sake and they could rule over everything.

It is very important to understand this, because it is the basis of the heretical and erroneous notion that the world, heaven forbid, is necessarily existent. Only God, may He be blessed, belongs to the category of necessary existence. All other things belong to the category of contingent existence.

When God created the world for Israel, His main intention was for Israel to carry out His original purpose and return to commune

with their original root.[2] In other words, the purpose of creation was
that Israel return and become an integral part of God, whose existence is necessary. As long as the people of Israel fulfill the divine
wish and commune with their root, which belongs to the category of
necessary existence, the whole world, which was created only for
Israel, is included in the same category of things whose existence is
necessary.

This end is the sole purpose for the creation of the world, and
because of this God is compelled, so to speak, to create and sustain
the worlds for Israel, as we have already explained, so that Israel can
fulfill His original plan, as we have also explained. Thus, the whole
world is included in the category of necessary existence precisely
and only when Israel fulfills God's wishes.

The more Israel fulfills God's wishes, the more Israel becomes
an integral unity with the worlds that are dependent on it for their
necessary existence; by doing more and more of the divine wishes.
Israel more and more becomes a part of God, whose existence is
necessary, and then all the worlds which are dependent on the souls
of Israel are included with the souls of Israel in the category of
necessary existence, as we have explained.

The way of negation[3] is the only means of achieving the purpose of returning and becoming an integral part of the divine
unity—of returning to and communing with the divine unity whose
existence is necessary. In order to become an integral part of the
divine unity, one must completely negate his own existence.

This state of negation can only be reached through solitude.
When an individual, in solitude, speaks directly to his Creator, he
may achieve negation of all his body's desires and evil inclinations
and finally reach the state of negating his material existence altogether so as to become an integral part of the divine root.

Solitude is most easily attained at night, when the world is free
from its everyday cares and concerns.[4] In the daytime, when we are
all pursuing our worldly needs, the world is too much with us,
becoming a source of confusion and distraction that prevents us
from communing with and becoming an integral part of God. Even
if you yourself are not preoccupied with worldly matters, everyone
else is, and this makes it difficult to achieve the state of negation.

Solitude should also be sought in a special place that is far from
human habitations, in a remote area not frequented by others.
True solitude and clarity of thought cannot be attained in a place
that people frequent during the daytime hours in pursuit of their

worldly needs, and this is so even when no one else is present. Therefore you should go alone at night to a place where you are unlikely to encounter anyone else, and there you must purge your heart and mind of everything that pertains to the material world, negating everything until you reach the category of complete negation.

At the outset you should pray a great deal and talk to God, in solitude, at night, in a remote place, until you manage to negate all your worldly desires and inclinations. Then proceed to increase your practice of solitude until you manage to negate all your other desires and evil inclinations. In this way, over an extended period in the same place at the same time, you will succeed in negating everything.

Even then, however, something of yourself still remains that must be negated until nothing at all remains.[5] This means [6] that after you have succeeded in negating all desires and evil inclinations, something of yourself may still remain to be negated, such as pride and material existence,[7] and therefore you still think of yourself as something. It is necessary to continue your effort to achieve total negation in solitude until nothing whatsoever of your personality remains, so that you become what you really should be— nothing—and reach the state of true negation.

Once you have attained negation, your soul will become an integral part of its source and root—that is, a part of Him whose existence is necessary, may be He blessed. Then all the world will become integrated within you with your soul and its divine root, whose existence is necessary, as we explained above. And as a result, due to you and your effort, as we have also explained above, the whole world will be included in the category of necessary existence.

(Source: *Likutey Moharan Kama*, chap. 52)

1. Literally *taut*, "mistake," which in Hebrew sounds like *dat*, "religion." This word was used to denote a false religion, a heresy, not just a mistake.

2. In kabbalistic usage, "root" means the specific divine, spiritual source of any created thing in the realm of the divine emanations. "Commune" (*le-davek*) means to be reunited spiritually with this source.

3. "Negation" (*bitul*) is the opposite of existence, used here, of course, in the spiritual sense (though historically it may have a cosmic meaning in Lurianic Kabbalah).

4. "The world" (*ha-olam*) here means the community, the social unit, or just "everybody," without any "cosmic" significance.

5. The idea of the solitary negation of all worldly attributes and the achievement of communion, and even unity, with God is described here as an individual experience, contrary to the usual Hasidic description of the interrelationship of the individual Hasid with his community and with the Zaddik. It is possible, however, that Rabbi Nahman is describing the way of the true Zaddik, of whom there is only one,

namely Rabbi Nahman himself. It is difficult to know whether the homily is norma-
tive, and therefore directed to all Hasidism, or an autobiographical account (either
factual or imaginary) of Rabbi Nahman's own religious experience. The cosmic
significance attached to the practices discussed in the homily tends to indicate that it
is an account of the Zaddik's role in the world rather than general instruction for the
ordinary Hasid's everyday religious life.

    6. These two explanatory sentences are not an integral part of Rabbi Nahman's
homily, but an explanation appended by the compiler, Rabbi Nathan, though very
probably not without Rabbi Nahman's knowledge and approval.

    7. *Gasut* should be interpreted here as "material" in the negative sense of the
word—the opposite of "pure" (*dak*) or spiritual.

SATAN, ISRAEL, AND THE EXILE

The Book of Lamentations begins with the words, "How doth the
city sit solitary that was full of people."[1] In discussing this verse, the
Alsheikh[2] observed that it would have been more appropriate to
begin with the suffering of the people than with the disaster to the
city. I recall that my teacher, the Besht,[3] told a parable that resolves
the difficulty raised by the Alsheikh. It went as follows.

    A Jewish merchant was once caught at sea in a storm that
threatened to sink his ship. He began to pray, begging God to save
him because of his wife's exceptional virtuousness. A gentile, who
happened to overhear, asked the merchant about his wife. When
the merchant replied that she was a paragon of fidelity and virtue,
the gentile boasted that he could seduce her. The two men made a
wager, agreeing that the wife would be proven unfaithful if the
gentile was able to bring the husband the ring she always wore.

    The gentile went to the merchant's house and tried to seduce
the wife. He returned several times, pretending to have a message
from the husband, but no matter how he tried, he got nowhere at
all. Finally he bribed the woman's maid to steal the ring. He took it
to the husband, and as they had agreed when they made their wager,
the merchant turned his whole cargo over to the gentile and returned home empty-handed.

    Meanwhile, when the woman learned that her husband was
home, she beautified herself and went to greet him, as usual, with
tender loving words. This time, though, much to the wife's puzzle-
ment, the husband seemed utterly indifferent to her. It was as if his
heart had not crossed the threshold when he entered the house.

Soon after this the husband arranged to send his wife away, putting her on a ship manned by only one sailor—actually himself disguised in seaman's clothing. After several days at sea with nothing to eat or drink, the wife asked the "sailor" for some food. "Only if you let me kiss you," he replied. She gave in because she had no choice. Later on he made her go to bed with him.

When the ship reached land, the "sailor" put the wife ashore. Searching for food, she found two trees, one of them bearing fruit that caused leprosy, the other, fruit that cured leprosy. The wife took some of the fruit and, disguised as a man, eventually arrived at a royal palace where she cured someone who was suffering from leprosy. She was rewarded with a great fortune.

Returning home, the wife encountered her husband. She angrily laced into him for the terrible things he had done to her— sending her away in a ship with a filthy, ugly sailor who had forced her to do all sorts of filthy, ugly things, and so on. The husband was secretly delighted by his wife's outrage and her complaints about the violation of her chastity. He made a few inquiries and quickly found out how the gentile had tricked him with a stolen ring and a false accusation. Now that everything was clear, he took vengeance on the gentile.

The meaning of this parable is also clear—it concerns everything that has happened and will happen from the destruction of the Temple until the coming of the Messiah, may it be soon, Amen. When the Besht's soul ascended to heaven, he saw how Michael, the great protector of Israel, defended Israel by maintaining that any sin Israel may commit is really a good deed. If Jews cheat a little, it is only in order to marry their daughters off to talmudic scholars or to have something to give to charity. Whatever they do is from necessity and not because of a wish to sin. Now regarding the parable, it is well known that a virtuous woman represents the Shekhinah, as is hinted in the verse that says, "A virtuous woman is a crown[4] to her husband" (Proverbs 12:4). The gentile is like Satan, who said, "The Jews are virtuous now, when they have a Temple and can offer sacrifices, but if you want to test them, destroy the Temple and then I will be able to seduce them." With the maid's help he stole the ring—this refers to the secret of the two goats—one for the Lord and one for Azazel, (Leviticus 16:8–10). And he sent her away in a ship—it is as if God changed Himself into the holy name SAL.[5] This is the secret meaning of the Shekhinah's complaints about how she was forced to submit, and so forth. And then it became clear that everything was a satanic lie, and then it is said: "For the Lord hath a sacrifice in Bozrah, and a great slaughter in the land of Edom" (Isaiah 34:6).

(Source: *Toledot Ya'akov Yosef: Shoftim*)

1. The parable in this homily is intended to demonstrate that Lamentations 1:1 is a foreshadowing of Israel's fate. The verse is not actually quoted in the original text of the homily, which begins with the question raised by the Alsheikh.

2. Rabbi Moses Alsheikh, the most prominent homiletical writer in sixteenth-century Safed and the author of *Torat Moshe*, a collection of homiles on the Torah, as well as many other books, covering most of the Bible. His homiletical observations are very often quoted by Rabbi Ya'akov Yosef.

3. Rabbi Israel Besht is quoted this way several hundred times in Rabbi Ya'akov Yosef's work.

4. "Crown" (*atarah*) is one of the usual symbols of the Shekhinah in kabbalistic terminology.

5. The letter-group SAL comprises one of the most holy secret names. When one letter is added, *mem*, it becomes Samael, the name of Satan. The text means that God disguised Himself by assuming Satan's name in order to try Israel and the Shekhinah during the exile (the ship), and that the coming of the Messiah, as well as the punishment of the gentiles, will be the final proof that the Shekhinah did not sin, and neither did Israel, which is what the Besht testified he had seen Michael prove in heaven.

ISRAEL AND THE ANGELS

There is another reason,[1] and it is explained by a parable. There were once some princes whom the king loved very much. They were always in his presence, had a complete understanding of his greatness, and continually praised and glorified him. After some time the princes left the king; they wandered far and wide, losing their way and becoming poor. Saddened because their rich clothing was tattered and they missed the king, they continued to wander, eventually becoming so encrusted with the dust of the road that they could barely remember their former pleasures and the king's greatness.

In time the princes were so hard pressed that they returned to the king's palace. When they arrived at the gate and once again became aware of the king's greatness, dignity, and glory, they were ashamed of themselves for ever having been so evil as to leave him. They were so embarrassed by their evil conduct and filthy clothing that they were unable to present themselves to the king, but at least they were wise enough to praise and glorify him again as they had in the past.

The princes begged the king to forgive them for their sins and to replace their filthy rags with new garments suitable for attending upon him and enjoying the pleasures of the court. The king had pity on his beloved children and did what they asked. Now they were once more able to see the king's face and to understand his greatness and glorify him.

The meaning of this parable is clear. We, the people of Israel, who are called children of God, left the Lord and wandered to a far-off place. Following a twisted road, we sinned and committed crimes, and our sins made us dirty. Now, on Rosh Hashanah, we return to God and are elevated before him, but our hearts are filled with sorrow because of our sins and evil deeds. We are ashamed because of the dirt that encrusts us and we are terrified by God's greatness and glory. Because of this fear, and because we are encrusted with the dirt of the streets, our sins, we do not have the wisdom to understand God's greatness and to glorify Him. So we plead with God to forgive our sins and crimes and to remove our filthy rags. Because of His great pity and charity, God is merciful; He forgives us and garbs us in a new spirit so that we can return to His worship with pure hearts. Then we are able to worship Him and acclaim Him and understand His greatness and sing songs of praise before Him.

(Source: *Kedushat Levi: Rosh Hashanah*)

1. This pericope is part of a longer homiletical discussion of a passage in the Talmud in which the angels ask why Israel does not sing before God on Rosh Hashanah (see B. Rosh Hashanah 32b).

MOURNING AND REDEMPTION

Tractate Taanit of the Talmud (30b) says that anyone who mourns for Jerusalem will merit seeing her in her joy. On the face of it this saying seems illogical. Does it mean that if you do not mourn, you will not be permitted to participate in the infinite goodness and ultimate perfection of the future era even if you have worshiped God all your life?

In order to understand this apparent contradiction it is necessary to understand what is meant by mourning. There are three reasons for us to mourn: the destruction of the Temple, the destruction of Jerusalem, and the exile of the people of Israel. There are two ways to understand mourning. The first and simpler way is as follows: When the Temple and Jerusalem and Zion were still standing, and Israel lived in its own country, all was in the state of ultimate perfection, and the divine flow of goodness, which provided existence to the world as a whole, was derived from above by our worship through the sacred service in the Temple and the sacrifices we offered there. Now that all this is lacking, we remain poor and empty, despised and lowly.

The second way of understanding mourning is for those who have secret knowledge. We mourn the exile of the Shekhinah because when the Temple and Jerusalem were standing, and Israel lived in its own country, there was divine revelation, and it was possible to worship and to perform the sacred service of the Temple. Since the divine revelation which was present in the Temple enabled us to understand the greatness of the Creator and the magnificence of His power, and to know that He had contracted His Shekhinah in the Temple,[1] we were able to cause the emanation of divine revelation and to achieve complete self-negation before God and His glory, worshiping Him with a happy heart and joyously performing the commandments and deeds of charity. Now that the Temple has been destroyed, however, this aspect of God's kingdom[2] has descended and donned mourning garments—this is the aspect of the exile of the Shekhinah, which is the congregation of Israel.

It is also necessary to mourn the aspect of Jerusalem, which means the aspect of total fear[3]—the disappearance of the fear of God and of self-negation before Him. The essence of mourning is to awaken ourselves, through the mourning rites and the sorrow in our hearts, so that we may purify our material bodies. When we remember the magnificence of the divine revelation in the days when the Temple was standing, and all the beauty and glory we enjoyed at that time, the soul inside us weeps and our hearts feel deep sorrow because of the absence of divine revelation, and through this process we are purified. Someday God will remember us to our benefit and will ingather all our exiles when our Messiah finally comes—may it be soon, Amen—and when this happens, we will then deserve the great sweetness, friendship, and joy which will be revealed at that time.

But if we do not mourn now, we will forget everything, and then we will be unable to accept the great light of that joy. Our material composition and earthly bodies will prevent us from fulfilling the verse in Isaiah that says: "For they shall see, eye to eye, the

Lord returning to Zion" (52:8). The following parable will make this clear.

There was once a prince who was always in the king's presence, where he was continually exposed to the king's greatness and magnificence and shared in the royal pleasures. But then the prince did something evil and the king ordered him driven away. Deprived of all the luxuries of the royal court, the prince became accustomed to a base, simple existence and almost completely forgot his earlier life. He knew in his heart, though, that the king was kind and forbearing and one day would forgive him and restore him to his former station. But, said the prince to himself, if the coarse habits of his present existence became ingrained, he would no longer be able to fit in at court when the king eventually forgave him. The prince was a clever youth, and he knew he had to prevent this from happening. In order to keep his old life alive in his memory, he decided to make it the central focus of his thoughts, continually contemplating it and mourning over what he had once known but then lost. By this means he counteracted the vulgarizing influence of his lowly life in exile. He was purified, as it were; his nature did not become crude and his lowly station did not lower him, for his mind was consistently fixed in contemplation of the life at court. His heart was always on fire with memories of the past and the desire once again to view the king's countenance and enjoy the pleasures of the royal court.

In the same way, by contemplating God's greatness and continually mourning the exile of the Shekhinah and the supreme fear, which is an aspect of Jerusalem, as was explained above, we purify ourselves of all earthly dross and material elements and thus become able to accept the divine revelation and the many pleasures and the great light that will come in the future.

Sinners will not be able to accept the light and the great pleasures that will come from the divine revelation because they have not counteracted their earthliness and their material nature by adopting the practice of contemplating the greatness of their Creator all the days of their exile. Instead they will be abolished and lost. But this will not be the lot of the righteous, who have purified themselves by continually contemplating the greatness of the Creator, mourning the exile of the Shekhinah, and constantly awaiting and looking forward to the coming of the Messiah, may it occur in our days, Amen. When the divine glory is revealed, and the divine light shines on them, they will bask in its delights. This is what they have been seeking, and they will be healed. And this is what our sages meant when they said in the Talmud that anyone who mourns for Jerusalem will see her greatness. One who keeps this constantly in mind, contemplating the greatness of the Creator, mourning the exile of the Shekhinah and the aspect of supreme fear, the aspect of Jerusalem, and purifying his soul—as we have explained—will deserve to see the joy of Jerusalem, for he will be a suitable vessel for the divine revelation, the divine light, and the great joy.

(Source: *Kedushat Levi: Likutim*)

1. This is the idea of the zimzum, which originated in the midrashic description of God concentrating Himself between the cherubim (Pesikta 152a and other places). For further discussion, see the Introduction.

2. "Kingdom" (*malchut*) is one of the more common symbols for the Shekhinah, as well as "Kneset Yisrael," the congregation of Israel.

3. Rabbi Levi Yitzhak breaks the word *yerusalayim* (Jerusalem) into two parts: *yare* ("fearful") and *shalem* ("complete").

THE COMMANDMENTS AND THE TORAH

There is a type of fear of God which is really fear of the commandments. When someone realizes that observing the commandments is a matter of divine moment, and begins to perform them with his physical limbs and other material "tools," he becomes fearful and spiritually agitated, for how can he materialize something divine? After all, is God material, heaven forbid? Once someone has experienced this fear and spiritual agitation several times, he begins to derive strength from his faith in God, because he knows that performing the commandments is a means of establishing a connection with God, since the commandments are the word of the Living God, coming from the Supreme Will which spoke and its will was done, and whose influence continues through all the descending stages, reaching its end in the stage of the lowly beings. He then understands that the Shekhinah is clothed in the commandment, because every commandment is an aspect of the Shekhinah, which is clothed in matter to make it possible for material, lowly beings to form a connection with God through the limbs with which they perform the commandments. This connection is achieved by the descending divine powers and the divine knowledge and wisdom,[1] whose original root reaches the Ein Sof.[2]

All this is shown by the verse that says, "For the commandment is a lamp, and the teaching is light" (Proverbs 6:23). The commandment is a lamp beside the Torah, which is light, because

Wisdom and Intelligence[3] are called "the light of the Torah." In other words, Wisdom and Intelligence enable a person to perform the commandment in order to illuminate it. By this means the commandment itself becomes a lighted lamp and gives light.

(Source: *Pri Ez: Noah*)

1. The author is referring to the third sefirah, Binah.
2. Ein Sof, the divine power above the sefirot, is beyond even symbolic description.
3. Hochmah and Binah, the second and third sefirot.

THE PURPOSE OF FOOD

We will now explain a great mystery. Why did God create various foods and beverages and cause man to desire them? Because every food and beverage contains a spark from the First Adam. The sparks entered into minerals, plants, animals, and human beings; they still reside there, and they have a great desire for communion with holiness. The sparks evoke the descent of divine emanation from above, as reflected in the proverb that "no drop descends from above unless two ascend in harmony with it."[1]

There is a divine spark that is a part of yourself in everything you eat and drink,[2] and it is your duty to restore it to its proper place. This is shown by the verse that says, "Hungry and thirsty, their soul fainted in them" (Psalms 107:5). One hungers and thirsts for the sparks. Why? Because "their soul fainted in them"; because, in the mystery of exile, he mistakenly thought she was a prostitute because she covered her face.[3] Similarly, all the things that serve man's human needs belong to the same structure as his soul, but they are clothed differently.

(Source: *Keter Shem Tov* I)

1. This is not a rabbinic saying but a later proverb.
2. The spark originated in the divine world in the same place from which the person's soul is derived. For further discussion see the Introduction.
3. See Genesis 38:15.

THE PURPOSE OF THE *GILGUL*

In his writings on the *gilgul* (transmigration of souls), the Ari of blessed memory[1] says that human beings are continually reborn through metempsychosis, each time in a new body, until all their sins and evil ways are corrected.[2]

. . . There has been considerable discussion and disagreement on the question of which body one will be renewed in at the time of the resurrection if he has undergone *gilgul* several times. The kabbalists, who study God's ways, usually maintain that he will be renewed in his original body, while the philosophers hold that it will be his last body. I take a moderate, in-between view. It is known that the 248 positive commandments are in harmony with the 248 limbs of the human body, while the 365 negative commandments are in harmony with the body's 365 sinews.[3] Each limb is in harmony with one particular commandment. We know this from the statement of our blessed sages in the Talmud (B. Yoma 28b) that Abraham was able to fulfill all the commandments even though he lived before the Torah was given because he was inspired with the whole Torah through his limbs.

When a person follows all the commandments in the Torah, he mends and completes the structure of his own body, both the 248 limbs and the 365 sinews. But if he sins and disobeys one of the commandments, he injures the limb that is connected to that commandment, becoming crippled as if he lacked that limb. Thus someone who disobeys a negative commandment or disregards a positive commandment injures himself and is crippled in the limb that is in harmony with the commandment he violates. In order to restore the perfection of his body's structure by healing his injured limbs, he must mend the commandments he has broken during the course of many *gilgulim*.

In the time of the resurrection, when God ingathers all the exiles of Israel, each Jew will have perfected the structure of his body and soul. All will be able to enter the king's palace without any limbs missing, for they will have gathered and mended their limbs through the healing and completing in each *gilgul*. The particular limbs which have been healed and renewed in each *gilgul* will be built into a new body, and when the individual has completed his cycle of *gilgulim*, his body will be complete and perfect in every way since it will be made up of these healed and completed limbs; nothing will be lacking.

(Source: *Kedushat Levi: Va-Ethanan*)

1. Rabbi Isaac Luria of Safed (1534–1572). See Introduction.

2. The author is referring to two extremely influential books on metempsychosis from the Lurianic school. *Sefer ha-Gilgulim* and *Sha'ar ha-Gilgulim*, both written by Rabbi Hayim Vital.

3. Positive commandments are filled by doing something; negative commandments are those that forbid something.

PART TWO

THE ZADDIK

THE ZADDIK'S FAITH

The Zaddik's righteousness is the source of faith, because the Zaddik only wants to please the Creator, his master. Since it is impossible to understand God except through the faith that there is One who created all, the Zaddik cannot pursue the purpose of pleasing God unless he can understand at least a small part of God's ways.

Therefore, as we learn from the verse that says, "Know thou the God of thy father and serve Him" (I Chronicles 28:9), the Zaddik's soul longs to know all of God's ways and to worship Him through this knowledge. In truth, faith is always higher than reason. Even though his reason has not yet arrived at an understanding of God, the Zaddik's perception of the Creator's greatness becomes greater and greater. He originally came to this awareness through faith, without understanding, and later began to understand it through his reason, by means of worship and the sacrifice of his soul . . . so that his faith is elevated to a higher plane. Once the Zaddik achieves this he returns to the world, and this process has no end, because faith finds its source in the Ein Sof.

(Source: *Pri Ez*, homily for Shabbat Teshuvah)

THE LINK WITH THE ZADDIK

"Then shall he and his neighbor next unto his house take one" (Exodus 12:4). Our books ask why it is that some people have a real sense of kinship with each other and like each other very much, and large numbers of people are sometimes willing to follow the lead of one man, whereas it also happens that people who have studied together sometimes have nothing to do with each other.

The answer, undoubtedly, is that those who like each other in this world sat next to each other in paradise. Since they were good neighbors there, they are also close to each other here. That is the meaning of "Then shall he and his neighbor next unto his house take one." In other words, here is a sign for determining whether someone is a Zaddik—do people draw close to him and dwell with him in complete love?

(Source: *Noam Elimelech: Bo*)

THE ZADDIK'S SIN

A Zaddik must establish communion with the people he wants to help if he is to influence them and draw down divine emanation for them. Anyone who wants to help a friend cannot do so properly unless he is in communion with his friend. Similarly, to help the people of Israel, a Zaddik must establish communion with them.

How should a Zaddik behave with people who are, heaven forbid, sinful? Even a wicked person cannot live without divine emanation, but how can a Zaddik establish communion with a wicked person? The answer is found in the talmudic passage that says, "Great is the sin which is committed for the sake of heaven" (B. Nazir 23b). The Zaddik too must commit a sin—but it is a sin for the sake of heaven.

(Source: *Noam Elimelech: Nasa*)

THE ZADDIK AND THE DANGER OF PRIDE

A great Zaddik, who has been righteous for a very long time and continually grows stronger in his righteousness, is not threatened by pride even though he has many notable achievements to his credit. On the contrary, he is still able to see his own defects and grieves because his worship is incomplete. Furthermore, his very efforts to help the people of Israel cause him pain, for deep within himself he feels the bitter suffering of their life in exile—the heavy taxation, and so forth—and because of his concern about the people of Israel, the enthusiastic joy he feels during worship and communion seems like nothing to him. Zaddikim like this are the pillars of the world of Israel.

But Zaddikim who are newcomers—who are just beginning their worship—become enthusiastic and proud when they accomplish something holy, and imagine that they have already arrived at the peak of true worship. Though they are Zaddikim, nonetheless they are guilty of the sin of pride.

(Source: *Noam Elimelech: Shemot*)

TWO KINDS OF ZADDIKIM

There are two kinds of Zaddikim. There is the Zaddik who does not care about the world and is not interested in what happens there. His worship is intended solely to purify and mend his own soul and uplift it to its source, the divine place from which it was originally taken.

The other kind of Zaddik, holy and pure, constantly worries and grieves because of the suffering of the people of Israel. All his thoughts and intentions are aimed at drawing divine emanations to benefit them.

(Source: *Noam Elimelech: Shemot*)

A ZADDIK SON OF A ZADDIK

There is a Zaddik who is a Zaddik because of the merits of his fathers or because he is always in the company of Zaddikim. This is not a matter for great concern, because the Zaddik who is the son of a Zaddik knows that he will not attain salvation by relying on his ancestry and the merit of his fathers. He is hardly likely to feel that he need not commit himself fully in worshiping God. Rather, he will commit himself to the worship of God with all his might.

As for the Zaddik who is not the son of a Zaddik, he will not fear that he cannot achieve true worship of God because he cannot rely on the merits of his fathers. Rather, he will worship God truly, for as it says in the Talmud, one who strives to purify himself

receives help from heaven (B. Shabbat 104a). He need only remember that God will help him.

(Source: *Noam Elimelech: Lech Lecha*)

THE ZADDIK AND RIGHTEOUSNESS

Charity *(zedakah)* is an act of the highest character.[1] Whoever gives
zedakah to the perfect Zaddik, who brings unity to the divine powers,
is performing a great and important act. There are two superior
divine powers: Zedek and Zedakah.[2] The Zaddik who receives
Zedakah can uplift the Shekhinah, the final *he*,[3] which is in exile
with us, to the power of Zedek, so that it becomes Zedakah (charity). When this happens the world will become full—no one will
hunger, all goodness will be present, along with multitudes of
blessings, charity, life, sons, and food/livelihood.[4] The whole world
will have peace, and everyone's needs will be provided.

(Source: *Noam Elimelech: Pequdey*)

1. *Zedakah*, the feminine form of *zaddik*, "righteous," has two meanings: "charity" and "righteousness." In the opening line of the homily its primary meaning is
"charity," referring to the contribution a Hasid gives to the Zaddik.
2. In kabbalistic symbolism, Zedek often represents Tiferet, the superior sefirah,
below which is the sefirah Yesod, or Zaddik, and below them the Shekhinah, or
feminine power, which is also represented by the symbol Zedakah, standing for
charity or righteousness.
3. The fourth letter of the holy name, *he*, is a symbol of the Shekhinah.
4. The last three items—life, sons, and food (or livelihood)—are often used as a
conventional formula describing the benefits the Hasid receives from the Zaddik.

THE ZADDIK'S MISSION

King Solomon said that "a righteous man falleth seven times and
riseth up again" (Proverbs 24:16). This saying pertains to the Zaddik, who succeeds in overcoming all the lowly desires that have no
supporting sustenance of their own, because everything that exists
has existence only in order to honor God, as is shown by what King
David said, "Thine, O Lord, is the greatness and the power" (I

Chronicles 29:11). In other words, the concept of God enters all the powers, and then fire goes before him and the sparks are uplifted. Now we can understand what is meant by "a righteous man falleth seven times." "Falleth" means causing their fall, because the righteous man—the Zaddik—breaks and lowers all seven lower powers by bringing the idea of God into them. As a result, they "rise up again," because all the sparks are uplifted. This process was the main purpose of creation, because God created existence from nothing so that the Zaddik would break the earthly powers and uplift them back to their original source.

(Source: *Pri Ha-Aretz: Lech Lecha*)

THE ZADDIK'S LIGHT

There is a Zaddik who is very famous and important in his own country, but not in a neighboring country, though he is also very famous in a third country. But the fact is that even in places where he is totally unknown and regarded as nothing, he is the medium by means of which the source of existence and life is received, for in such places he is present but invisible, as is indicated by the passage in the Zohar (III 280a) that tells how a spring arises in one place, then goes underground, and then surfaces somewhere else, but waters the roots of the holy tree even when it is flowing underground.

The Holy Torah and the true Zaddikim give light to all the worlds—a great light, a light which is thousands and tens of thousands of times more brilliant than this world and all its vanities—but people are so deeply immersed in the vanities of this world, and their purview is so limited, that they think there is nothing better. Though this world is small and insignificant, and nothing in it is real, it stands before their eyes and prevents them from seeing the great and holy light of the Torah and the true Zaddikim. When you hold a small coin before your eyes, you cannot see a huge mountain even though the mountain is thousands and tens of thousands of times larger than the coin. Similarly, this negligible little world in which we live, and the desire in this world for coins and money, stands before a person's eyes and prevents him from seeing the great light of the Torah and the Zaddikim.

If, however, you realize that you are prevented from seeing such great lights only because something so small and insignificant is blocking your view, then it is easy to remove the world from before your eyes and not look at it. Instead, lift your head, raise your eyes, and look at something higher than this world, and if you do so, you will immediately be able to see the great, boundless light of the Torah and the true Zaddikim, just as you were able to see the mountain as soon as you removed the coin. As the holy Besht of blessed memory said, "Woe, the world is full of very wonderful lights and secrets, and a small hand covering your eyes prevents you from seeing them."

(Source: *Kitzur Likutey Moharan* 132-133)

OBEDIENCE TO THE ZADDIK

The main principle and the basis of everything is to connect yourself to the Zaddik of the generation, accepting whatever he says, whether important or unimportant, and never sidestepping from what he tells you, neither to right nor to left, heaven forbid.

Purge your mind of all that you have learned of the secular sciences, and fill it, as if you had no mind of your own, only with the knowledge you receive from the Zaddik, the true rabbi. As long as you retain even a tiny bit of your own mind, you are not completely connected to the Zaddik.

In the same way, the main principle of Israel's acceptance of Torah was that they abandon whatever they had learned until then and believe only in God and in his servant Moses.

(Source: *Kitzur Likutey Moharan* 123)

THE ZADDIK'S WARNING

I heard the following parable from my teacher, the Besht. Once upon a time two travelers were passing through a forest where a band of robbers had their hideout. One of the men was as drunk as Lot;[1] the other was sober and fully in command of himself. The robbers attacked the two men, took everything they had, and beat them severely, leaving them barely alive. Later on, other travelers asked the two men whether they had gotten through the forest safely. The drunk one didn't know what to answer. The sober one warned them to be careful, explaining in great detail that there were robbers in the forest, that it was necessary to be well armed, and so forth. To put it briefly, the sober one was able to give a coherent, precise answer, while the drunk hadn't the slightest idea of what to say.

The same applies to the Zaddik who worships God. He knows about the robbers that threaten worshipers of God, he knows how dangerous the Evil Desire is, and he knows how to take precautions to avoid the ambushes laid by the evil powers. He lives in sorrow, but he knows how to warn others about the danger of the robber, "for in much wisdom is much vexation, and he that increaseth knowledge increaseth sorrow" (Ecclesiastes 1:18). The sinner, on the other hand, heedlessly indulges in the pleasures engendered by the Evil Desire, blithely maintaining that everything is fine because there is no danger in the world, and so forth.

(Source: *Toledot Ya'akov Yosef: Tavo*)

1. "Drunk as Lot" (See Genesis 19:32–35) is the rabbinic term for a state of intoxication in which one is conscious but no longer rational or responsible.

COMMUNION WITH THE ZADDIK

(a) If you wish to achieve communion with the true Zaddik,[1] know that whatever happens to him is intended for the Hasid's benefit. If you know this you can achieve a degree which is similar to the Garden of Eden by making confession before a scholar. By making confession you will know that whatever happens to him throughout his life is for your benefit, because God, who loves you, is the source of everything. If you have true knowledge, the circumstantial experiences of your life will not confuse you or cause you to rebel, because you will understand that whatever happens is part and parcel of the eternal good that is intended for you.

(b) By confessing before a true scholar, you raise the aspect of Malchut of the holy side[2] to its source, and by this means you destroy the suzerainty of the heathen on earth.[3] Thus you will gain the knowledge that whatever happens to you is for your own benefit and that you should bless God, who does only good, for this degree is like that of the Garden of Eden.

(c) The power of the true Zaddik is the source of the *tikkun* of all misdeeds.[4] If you wish to inherit everlasting life in the hereafter, try with all your might to draw close to the true Zaddikim and their disciples. And tell the Zaddik everything that is in your heart, making a full confession. Your sins will be absolved if you do this. Every sin is symbolized by a certain group of letters,[5] and when you sin this group of bad letters is engraved on your bones—the same letters that are used in the Torah to state the prohibition of whatever it was that you did. Thus, when you sin you join the letters of this prohibition to the evil powers,[6] entangling the holy Malchut in the exile of the evil powers. To prevent the evil engraving on your bones from taking revenge, confess before a scholar, so that the letters can be removed from your bones and a complete tikkun can be achieved.[7]

(Source: *Likutey Etzot, Teshura*, A)

1. The term "true Zaddik" is usually used by Rabbi Nahman of Bratslav and his disciples to denote Rabbi Nahman himself, and to differentiate between him and other Zaddikim. The terms "scholar" and "true scholar" in this passage seem to denote either Rabbi Nahman himself or one of his close disciples.

2. That is, the holy Shekhinah, which is threatened by the evil powers and may be captured by them because of the sins of a Jew. There is a similar divine aspect on the evil side, a kind of "evil Shekhinah," and that is why the text emphasizes the "holy Shekhinah."

3. According to Lurianic Kabbalah, based upon certain concepts in early Kabbalah, the Shekhinah is in exile and threatened by the powers of evil. Its source is its rightful place on the divine ladder of the sefirot, usually referring to a communion with the sefirah Tiferet, the male principle, which is described as the husband of the Shekhinah in kabbalistic symbolism.

4. According to Lurianic Kabbalah, the *tikkun*, or mending, of the catastrophe that occurred in the divine world is achieved by righteousness and obedience to the Jewish precepts. Here the Zaddik has a major role in achieving the tikkun.

5. The letters of the Hebrew alphabet, which were used by God when writing the Torah, are holy; by sinning human beings can transform their divine power into a source of power for Satan.

6. Thus giving more power to Satan, who takes the divine emanation in the holy letters and transforms them into evil deeds.

7. The classical idea of repentance, which in medieval Judaism was regarded as a spiritual contact between man and God, is achieved here by the Zaddik, who serves as an intermediary and is the principle power working toward achieving the tikkun. It is uncertain whether the term "complete tikkun" should be understood here as a reference to the individual sins of the confessing Hasid, or whether it has cosmic implications in the traditional Lurianic sense.

THE ZADDIK'S MYSTICAL STATUS

There is great value in having a close relationship with the True Zaddikim. Through such a relationship you can achieve complete repentance and forgiveness for your sins, so that the *dinim*[1] are sweetened and completely abolished. By this means, a union is established between God and the Shekhinah.[2]

The Holy Zohar on the verse "For lo, the kings assembled themselves" (Psalms 48:5) states that the two holy divine worlds—the upper divine world and the lower divine world—become one, and when they are united all the divine faces glow brightly and all sins are abolished (Zohar I, 206b). The divine wisdom has two aspects: upper wisdom and lower wisdom.[3] The lower divine wisdom is emanated from the upper wisdom, from which it derives its sustenance. The relationship is like that between a rabbi and a disciple. What the rabbi teaches the disciple, and what the disciple learns, is an aspect of the relationship between the upper wisdom and the lower wisdom.

Upper wisdom, which is what the rabbi teaches his disciple, is an aspect of the letter *yod*. What the disciple learns, which is an aspect of the lower widsom, is the aspect of the letter *lamed*, which is an aspect of "a tower floating in the air."[4] This is because the disciple's heart is floating in the air and hears what the rabbi is saying, and this is how a person listens and understands. The basis of the disciple's understanding is in his heart, for the rabbi has to say things that his heart will accept. The disciple, in turn, has to "give his heart"—to pay attention and observe what the rabbi has said—as is indicated in the verse that says, "To buy wisdom, seeing he [the fool] hath no understanding" (Proverbs 17:16).[5] Thus, what the disciple receives is an aspect of *lamed*, and an aspect of a "tower floating in the air." The aspect of *lamed*, then, means a disciple learning from the rabbi.[6] Thus, the rabbi and the disciple—aspects, respectively, of the upper wisdom and the lower wisdom— are aspects of the letters *lamed yod*.

The entire holy Torah is an aspect of the upper divine wisdom, while all other fields of knowledge in the world are derived from the aspect of the lower wisdom. When the fields of knowledge that derive from the lower wisdom are separated from the Torah and from God, and from the upper wisdom—like the disciple who does not want to understand his rabbi's teachings—this is an aspect of the diminishing of the moon,[7] in other words, of the exile of the Shekhinah.

Wherever you may be, it is necessary for you to establish a connection between your mind, from the place where you are, to the Torah and to God—to the aspect of the divine upper wisdom. But if, heaven forbid, you separate your mind and wisdom from God, this is the aspect described in the verse that says, "And a whisperer separateth familiar friends" (Proverbs 16:28).[8] In other words, he separates the ruler of the worlds and causes diminishing of the moon, heaven forbid, because he does not unite the lower wisdom with the upper wisdom, that is, he does not connect the worldly fields of knowledge to God and the Torah—the aspect of the upper divine wisdom, as was explained above.

The True Zaddikim unite the lower wisdom with the upper wisdom. The conversation of the True Zaddikim, even when they are talking about everyday things, is very precious, as our sages of blessed memory indicated when they said: "The conversation of learned men is something that should be studied" (B. Avodah Zarah 19b; B. Sukkah 21b).

Through his conversation and stories, and what he says to the common people, the True Zaddik rebuilds the destroyed worlds, lifting the lower wisdom and uniting it with the upper wisdom. Ordinary people are separated from the upper wisdom because they do not connect their minds to God, but the True Zaddik brings about this connection. He is even able to connect an evil person's mind and wisdom to God, and this is why Zaddikim talk to people whose behavior is far from perfect, and even to gentiles. When a Zaddik talks to a gentile, he brings out the good that is in him and the latter remains empty; this is the deep meaning of Moses killing the Egyptian.[9]

When the Zaddik talks to wicked people, he lifts up his own mind and unites it to God, and then he also uplifts their minds, from wherever they are, and connects them to God. The True Zaddik brings sinners to repentance by lowering his mind[10] and speaking to them with wonderful wisdom and great artistry, connecting all these conversations to God. True Zaddikim sometimes discuss wars and other worldly matters with wicked people, but the True Zaddik transforms these conversations, making them into a garment within which the great light of the Torah is found. Since he uses many different garments to clothe the Torah, he uses these as well, garbing the Torah's light in many different combinations. If the Zaddik immediately began talking about Torah with a wicked person, that person might become even more wicked and even more heretical. As the prophet says, "For the ways of the Lord are right, and the just do walk in them, but the transgressors do stumble therein" (Hosea 14:10). "For if he is lucky[11] it becomes like the elixir of life for him, but if he is not, it is like poison" (B. Yoma 72b). If the Torah were revealed to him as it is, it would be like poison for him, and his heresy would be reinforced. Since he is far away from the Torah, it must be presented to him in other combinations.

. . . We find, therefore, that the true Zaddik unites the upper wisdom with the lower wisdom. That is why God grieves when the Zaddik, heaven forbid, leaves the world, because God wants sinners to repent, not to die and be punished. It is the Zaddik who connected them with God, uplifting them toward Him and causing them to repent completely, because as we have explained, he is the one who brings about unity between the upper wisdom and the lower wisdom.

(Source: *Likutey Moharan II*, chap. 71)

1. *Dinim*, literally "judgments," are the spiritual consequences of sin—the evil powers generated by human sins.

2. Rabbi Nahman is referring here, and in the subsequent passage (the quotation from the Zohar), to the mystical union in the divine world between the male and female aspects, the sefirot Malchut and Tiferet.

3. Since there is an aspect of "wisdom" in every sefirah, this division does not necessarily refer to two specific sefirot. Rabbi Nahman's point is that there is a division between the lower and upper parts of the divine world, and it should be bridged, as he states below.

4. This expression is mentioned in B. Hagigah 15b as an example of a subject from which many *halakhot* can be derived. Rashi, giving one of the explanations current in his time, says that the expression refers to the Hebrew letter *lamed*, which is shaped like a high tower.

5. In the Hebrew text the word for "understanding" is *lev*, literally "heart."

6. The literal meaning of the word *lamed* is "one who learns."

7. The moon is a kabbalistic symbol for the Shekhinah. The diminishing of the moon means the separation of the Shekhinah and her husband.

8. In the Hebrew text *aluf* (instead of "familiar friends"). This word is interpreted by Rabbi Nahman (and others) as a reference to *alufo shel olam*, the Ruler of the World.

9. This last sentence is probably an addition by Rabbi Nathan.

10. Rabbi Nahman here uses the term *mezamzem*, literally: "contracts or diminishes his mind." In this he follows other Hasidic thinkers who connected the Lurianic concept of the zimzum with a benevolent attempt of the High to relate to the Lowly.

11. *Zachah* in Hebrew means "lucky" in a religious sense; that is, if his deeds, or the deeds of his father, justify it.

THE ZADDIK AS THE SOURCE OF ALL

Since all emanations[1] and all things come only from the true Zaddik, anyone who is close to the true Zaddik receives whatever he needs without any trouble, whether wealth or children. But someone who is far from the Zaddik acquires whatever he gets only with great difficulty.

This is so because the giving of wealth and children is determined by one's star,[2] and the star receives emanation from the Zaddik, who is the source of all emanations. When someone is far from the Zaddik, the star needs great strength to receive the Zaddik's emanation. As a result, occurrences of many different kinds take place. For example, someone may be given wealth and then die because of it, so that the wealth is given to his heirs; someone else may not only die when he receives wealth but also lose it; and so on. It is like what happens when someone tries to lift a heavy weight. By using all his strength, he may succeed in lifting it, but in the process, because of the great effort, he may also tear his intestines and die as a result; even so, he may still manage to hold on to the weight, but if he drops it, as may also happen, he dies because he lifted the weight and nothing remains in his grasp for his sons.

The same idea applies to wealth, because the star is so distant from the Zaddik that it needs great strength to receive emanation from him, and thus many different occurrences may take place. But if one is near the Zaddik, his star does not have to make such a great effort.

It is sometimes possible to lose your fortune even though you draw close to the true Zaddik. This happens because you see something very high and precious, or your star sees it even if you don't (B. Megillah 3a). When your star sees something very high and precious, it throws away your wealth, just as a man carrying a load of brass, who suddenly sees some gold and precious stones, will throw away the brass and run to pick up the more valuable things. Upon drawing close to the Zaddik, the star sees something more valuable than gold and pearls and throws away the wealth as if it were nothing. Even more so, someone who feels the Zaddik's nearness realizes that it is more precious than all the wealth in the world and then no longer cares about money and has no desire whatsoever for wealth.

(Source: *Likutey Moharan* I, 240)

1. *Hashpaot,* "emanations," also means "influences," which explains the astrological framework.

2. *Mazal,* both a star in the astrological sense and "luck."

THE ZADDIK'S INFLUENCE

Meeting the true Zaddik is a very great achievement.[1] While actually hearing the true Zaddik tell a homily is certainly an attainment of a high degree, seeing him without hearing a homily—simply being in the Zaddik's presence—is also very good. By seeing yourself with the Zaddik you receive greatness. The essence of greatness is humility, and this is true even of God, for as the Talmud tells us, "Wherever you find God's greatness, there you will find His humility" (B. Megillah 31a).

The degree of humility that we achieve as individuals is the essence of the future resurrection, when the dead will rise and live forever, because it is our humility that will be resurrected and brought back. We know this from the verse that says, "Awake and sing, ye that dwell in the dust" (Isaiah 26:19), because, as our blessed sages have explained, this verse refers to him "who dwelt near the dust during his life" (B. Sotah 5a). The essence of the future resurrection will pertain only to the element of humility, for it is the humility of each and every person that will be resurrected.

In the present era we cannot fathom the joys of the next world because we live within boundaries, and anything that is limited by boundaries cannot grasp the boundless spiritual joy of the next world. This also applies to the joy of the Sabbath, because to a certain extent the joy of the Sabbath resembles the joy of the next world, and for this reason our blessed sages said that whoever enjoys the Sabbath is given an unlimited share in the world to come (B.

Shabbat 118a; compare B. Berakhot 57b), a share without bound-aries. The joy of the Sabbath, like the joy of the next world, has the quality of boundlessness.

As the essence of the eternal life in the next world, boundless-ness is characterized by humility and humbleness. This is so be-cause the essence of boundlessness is the utter, total, and unlimited negation that can only be attained by those who have pushed them-selves to the utmost limits of humility. Thus the essence of the eternal life in the next world—the joy of the next world—will only be given to each person's humility.

. . . There is a general mind, and there are personal minds. All the personal minds receive from the general mind, which is the mind of the generation,[2] and this is the high degree achieved by those who merit seeing themselves together with the true Zaddik, because he is the wise man of the generation, the aspect of the general wise man, as was stated above. When the general wise man sees you and looks at you, your mind sparkles, and in consequence, through this sparkling of your mind, you receive greatness. As was explained above, this sparkling of the mind is the essence of great-ness. We know that it is transmitted by means of the faculty of seeing because, as Rashi has explained, wisdom is what is referred to by the word "eyes" in the verse that says, "And the eyes of both of them were opened" (Genesis 3:7).

When you look at the wise man who is the general mind, his power causes the light of wisdom and minds[3] to spring up inside you, and your mind sparkles. In this way you receive greatness, as was explained above. Each of us has a degree of mind and knowl-edge corresponding to our personal spiritual status, but the minds and knowledge of all of us rest in a lowly position[4] and do not sparkle. When the wise man of the generation looks at you, since he is the general mind, your mind sparkles, according to its special degree. Through this sparkling of your mind, you receive a degree of greatness corresponding to your mind's status. This sparkling of the mind is the source of greatness.

. . . The existence of a true leader, an aspect of Moses,[5] who knows simply by looking at someone how much greatness he is entitled to, makes it possible for each person to be allotted exactly the degree of greatness that he deserves. Once this happens, every ruler and leader of Israel, exactly to the extent that he deserves on the basis of his mind's status, will know how to formulate new interpretations of the Torah. When each person has been assigned to his rightful station—that is, when each person has exactly the degree of power and greatness he deserves, as we explained above—then each person will know, to an extent commensurate with his station and his degree of greatness, how to interpret the Torah and reveal new truths about it, and before how many people he should propound these innovative interpretations.[6] For example, he who is in charge of a thousand Jews—the prince of a thousand—has to propound Torah before a thousand people, and so on for all the others.

In each of these leaders, and in the true leader of all Israel, who is an aspect of Moses, there is an aspect of spirituality, as we learn from Rashi's interpretation of the verse "A man in whom is spirit" (Numbers 27:18). Rashi said: "He can treat everyone according to his spirit," meaning that all receive from him because he is the aspect of the general spirit, the aspect of "Thus saith the Lord God: Come from the four winds, O breath" (Ezekiel 37:9).[7] This spirit is an aspect of the divine spirit, which is closely related to the supreme minds, as indicated in the verse that says, "And I have filled him with the spirit of God, in wisdom and in understanding and in knowledge" (Exodus 31:3),[8] that is, with the aspect of the minds—the aspect of the worksmanship of the Temple.

One can only reveal innovative interpretations of the Torah to the extent that he is animated by the divine spirit, which is an aspect of the holy spirit, a spirit of prophecy. This divine spirit hovers over the Torah, as indicated by: "And the spirit of God hovered over the face of the waters" (Genesis 1:2), because as our sages of blessed memory explained, "waters" refers to the Torah.[9] Through the power of this divine spirit, one may merit to offer innovative interpretations of the Torah because, as was explained, the divine spirit hovers over the face of the Torah.

The power of the true leader, who is an aspect of Moses and an aspect of the general mind, influences the sparkling of each person's mind, which in itself is emanated and influenced by an aspect of the divine mind, because the divine spirit, as we have explained, is itself the higher minds. Through this process, each person is influenced with the ability to propound innovative Torah interpretations that come by means of the divine spirit which hovers over the face of the Torah, the aspect of the higher minds. All of this emanates from the leader who is an aspect of Moses and an aspect of the general mind or general spirit, as was explained above.

This leader has to practice a very high degree of *perishut*[10] and must live in great sanctity, for only then can he be a leader of Israel. His *perishut* and sanctity enable him to know how much greatness to allot to each of the people of Israel simply by looking at them, for such looking is dependent upon sanctity and a high degree of *perishut*.

. . . Therefore the leader must sanctify himself by means of *perishut*, purging himself of desire and purifying the eyes through which he will look at each person and provide him with the greatness he deserves simply by the power of his looking at him. Only then can he be a leader of Israel. When Israel does not have such a leader and observer, the whole world is immersed in confusion, and anyone who wants to use the holy name does so, as is the situation today because of our sins. The people of Israel need an observer who will watch them and see that each of them is assigned to his true station. This observer must be a *parush* and a great saint, from the standpoint of the sanctity and *perishut* of Moses; if he is, he can lead Israel and give everyone the greatness he deserves by looking at him, as we have explained above.

In this way *teshuvah* (repentance) is achieved, for the essence of repentance is shame. The leader, who shares the divine aspect of Moses, looks at each individual, causing his mind to sparkle. Thus, the people merit innovative understandings of the Torah, and in consequence they are overcome by shame, because they are now able to see how ashamed they ought to be. Beyond any shadow of a doubt, sin is very shameful. Sinning does not befit Israel, and it is improper for any member of the Jewish people to sin, heaven forbid. The same idea, however, also applies to *mitzvot* (good deeds). Anyone who wants to perform a *mitzvah* should be ashamed of his audacity in thinking he has a right to perform it. How dare he enter the king's palace to perform a mitzvah? The mitzvot are precious beyond imagining. If you focus your thoughts on Him before whom you are presenting the mitzvah and on the mitzvah's high spiritual value,[11] you will be ashamed to approach a mitzvah with intentions of fulfilling it. Look at yourself and see how far you are from God; then you will realize how audacious it is to take upon yourself the right to perform that mitzvah. Someone who has a true and appropriate sense of shame would even be ashamed to put food in his mouth, because whoever eats what is not rightfully his cannot face himself,[12] and if you have no right to the food you eat, and thus are eating what is not really yours, you should be profoundly ashamed. You should even be ashamed to lift the food to your mouth. The essence of shame, however, is derived from the leader who shares the aspect of Moses, because he brings the emanation of the interpretation of Torah to each individual, in this way providing each individual with a sense of shame.

. . . Fear of God and shame are the essence of repentance from the aspect of the Sabbath and from the aspect of eternal life in the next world, as was explained above. Each individual's humility is the essence of eternal life, for each individual's humility is the element that will be revivified in the process of resurrection. By means of repentance, the aspect of eternal life in the next world, the humbleness of Moses, will be resurrected, and this element is present in each limb of our bodies.

The aspect of the humbleness of Moses is present in every limb of every Jew. Moses caused his humbleness to emanate and enter every limb of every member of the people of Israel during the revelation at Mount Sinai. But the humbleness of Moses, though it is present and deeply rooted in every Jew, is passive. It is hidden within us and does not rise and reveal itself.

The humbleness of each person, however, will be resurrected by the power of the repentance that is the aspect of eternal life in the world to come. It is the essence of the resurrection, for at that time it will be resurrected. Thus, the humbleness of Moses will return and be resurrected, because it is rooted in every limb of every Jew. Before, it was hidden and covered, as if dead; now repentance causes it to return and awaken, and it is resurrected, because repentance is the aspect of eternal life, as we have explained, and humbleness—the aspect of every person that will rise at that time—is the essence of eternal life in the world to come. When each person's individual humbleness is resurrected—the essence of the humbleness of Moses which is embodied in every one of our limbs—then, by the light of the humbleness of Moses which has been revealed and resurrected within himself, every person will be able to see and feel his own humbleness.

. . . The rule to be derived from all this is that anyone who comes to the true Zaddik and hears Torah from him will be entitled by right to be enveloped by an emanation of great humbleness and shame. Indeed, the emanation of shame and humbleness upon him would be proof that he has seen a true Zaddik.

(Source: *Likutey Moharan* II, chap. 72)

1. Rabbi Nahman consistently says *lireot et azmo,* "to see oneself with the Zaddik," rather than "to meet."

2. In Rabbi Nahman's usage, "wise man of the generation" and similar appellations are almost synonymous with "True Zaddik."

3. Rabbi Nahman uses the word *mohin*, literally "minds," but actually a kabbalistic term denoting the higher spiritual elements of the divine world and the human psyche.

4. *Katnut*, "smallness," opposed to the "greatness" provided by the Zaddik.

5. Moses here is a symbol of a divine power. (An omitted section of the homily describes his leadership in the same terms.)

6. Rabbi Nahman is defining the relationship between the True Zaddik and the other Zaddikim of the same generation. The method described defines the size of the communities which they are allowed to lead.

7. In the Hebrew "wind" and "breath" are both called *ruah*, "spirit."

8. The terms used in this verse, "wisdom" (*hochmah*), "understanding" (*binah*), and "knowledge" (*da'at*), are symbols of the higher sefirot, which are also called "minds" of the divine body, as well as the human *mohin*, the higher element of the human spirit and mind.

9. B. Ta'anit 7a and many other talmudic and midrashic passages.

10. *Perishut* (literally: "being apart, separated") has several meanings in the ethical literature. Here Rabbi Nahman is apparently emphasizing the leader's loneliness and his separation from socialization and worldly affairs. This is contrary to the usual conception of the Zaddik's behavior but corresponds to what we know about Rabbi Nahman's personal life and inclinations.

11. The kabbalists interpreted the *mitzvot* as symbols of the higher sefirot, containing elements of divine truth; performing them, therefore, brings a person into close contact with God.

12. Rabbi Nahman is quoting a saying in the Jerusalem Talmud, Orlah, chap. 1.

REPENTANCE AND THE ZADDIK

The Zaddik has to make *teshuvah* for Israel.[1] When one of the people of Israel strays beyond the boundaries of the law, casting off the yoke of the *halakhah*, the Zaddik is compelled to make teshuvah for him. The parable that follows will explain this.

Once upon a time two men were traveling together. At first the horse that was pulling their carriage was calm enough, but suddenly it went wild, rocking them back and forth. One of the men began pummeling the horse with his fist. The other man laughed, "Do you think you can make an impression on a horse that way? All you're doing is hurting your own hand. Use a whip if you want to beat the horse." The first man did as the second advised. He whipped the horse so hard that it bolted and overturned the carriage, careening both of the men into the mud. Since that approach had not worked, the second man advised his colleague to tie the horse to a tree and then to beat it again until it learned a lesson. The first man did so, beating the horse until he was exhausted, but he saw that this course of action was no good either, because the horse wasn't worth all the trouble and exhaustion. The only way to handle the horse would have been to shoot him, but this the man did not want to do.

The situation is the same when a person sins, straying beyond the bounds of the halakhah and behaving improperly. There is nothing you can do about it and no foolproof advice to follow. Anyone could punish the sinner directly, or by means of a messenger,[2] or in some other way, but all punishments touch the Zaddik himself, just as they touch God, for as Isaiah says, "In all their afflictions He was afflicted" (Isaiah 63:9). They are all a part of the divine entity, and when something afflicts them, heaven forbid, He is afflicted too, so to speak. It is the same with the Zaddik, as shown by the verse that says, "to punish also the righteous [Hebrew: *zaddik*] is not good" (Proverbs 17:26), because any punishment that is meted out touches the Zaddik himself.

Man was created by four elements—fire, air, water, and earth—and all of these are drawn from one basic, simple element—the divine category of the Zaddik, as is shown by the verse that says, "the righteous is an everlasting foundation" (Proverbs 10:25).[3] In other words, the Zaddik belong to the category of the elemental, basic element[4] from which the other four elements are drawn, as we can see from the verse that says, "And a river went out of Eden to water the garden, and from thence it was parted and became four heads" (Genesis 2:10). "A river went out of Eden" is the category of the Zaddik, the element of the world, the category of the basic element from which the four elements—that is, the "four heads" in the verse—are drawn. Thus, all of the elements are drawn from the Zaddik, and that is why the Zaddik himself is affected when one of them is punished, and why "to punish also the Zaddik [righteous] is not good."

The authors of works on ethics have already explained this,[5] noting that when people come to see the Zaddik, in the sense indicated by the verse that says, "But thine eyes shall see thy teacher" (Isaiah 20:20), it is necessary for them to find themselves within the Zaddik, for by seeing the Zaddik's face, they can perceive all the ethical ways and how the Zaddik lives by them. The ethical ways are all drawn from those four elements. When you see the Zaddik, who is the category of the basic element from which all the other elements are drawn, you will gain an awareness that you too are attached to all the ethical ways that derive from the four elements that come from the Zaddik, who is their elementary source.

(Source: *Likutey Moharan* II, chap. 66)

1. "Making *teshuvah*" is more comprehensive than "repenting" because it includes the positive halakhic and ethical precepts connected with repentance.

2. It is unclear here whether the hypothetical punisher is God Himself, the Zaddik, or every Jew; the second possibility seems closest to the meaning of the whole passage.

3. The meaning of this verse in this context is lost in the translation. In Hebrew, literally: "The Zaddik is the element of the world."

4. The "element" here (translated "foundation" in the preceding biblical verse) refers to the ninth sefirah in the kabbalistic system, which is called (using this very verse) both Yesod (= element, foundation) and Zaddik.

5. Rabbi Nahman is referring here not only to the traditional writings on ethics but also to the Hasidic ethical teachings, both oral and in books.

LEADERSHIP AND REDEMPTION

Search long and hard for a true leader, and when you find one draw close to him,[1] because every leader has an aspect of[2] the spirit of prophecy. Even in our day, when prophecy has ceased, the leader has an aspect of "another spirit"[3] that is not found among ordinary people, and it is because of this spirit that he was destined for leadership. If it were otherwise, anyone could be a leader.

Indeed, every leader of Israel has the aspect of "another spirit" because a leader is an aspect of the "man of spirit"[4] who directs the people's comings and goings. It is because of this that he was destined to be a leader of Israel.

The leader's "other spirit" is an aspect of the holy spirit—the spirit of prophecy. Even though prophecy itself has ceased, he undoubtedly has an aspect of "another spirit" which derives[5] from the sacred and is not found in ordinary people. This too is an aspect of the holy spirit; while it is not actually the holy spirit that makes knowledge of the future possible, it is an aspect of the holy prophetic spirit.

The true leader's aspect of the holy spirit, which is an aspect of the prophetic spirit, strengthens and improves[6] the faith of all who draw close to him, the faith derived from the holy truth in the divine world. The aspect of imagination in everyone who succeeds in drawing close to the true leader is purified and improved by the power of the leader's aspect of the power of prophecy.[7]

This aspect of the prophetic spirit is the major power that can mend the power of imagination, and when the imagination is mended, as we said above, the holy faith is improved and purified. Thus, those who draw close to the true leader receive a pure faith that is directly derived from the holy.

To find such a leader, you must search long and hard, and if you want to be granted an opportunity to draw close to such a true leader, in order to receive true faith in a complete way, you must ask God's help. If you should draw close to a false leader, heaven forbid, you will be on the way to false faith, because a false leader is an aspect of the false prophet, an aspect of a false spirit,[8] and through him your imagination will become evil, bringing on false beliefs.

The true leader's aspect of the prophetic spirit, which purifies the imagination so that faith is improved, is the basis for correcting faith, as we have said. If the aspect of prophecy is not present, so that your imagination cannot be purified and mended, you will become confused, and your mind will be a hodgepodge of good and evil mixed with false beliefs. This is an aspect of the snake's venom,[9] because befuddling the imagination and confusing it with false beliefs is an aspect of the dirt of the snake. Magicians and diviners work by the power of an unmended, impure imagination; they are befuddled and confused with false beliefs, the lies and nonsense that are the dirt of the snake. But the effects of the dirt of the snake were removed from the people of Israel[10] when they stood at Mount Sinai and gained the power of prophecy by means of the power of Moses, their true leader and greatest prophet. When their power of imagination was mended and purified, and they gained true faith in the Lord, the venomous dirt of the snake—the poison of false beliefs—was removed from them, and by purifying the imagination, they gained complete, unimpeded faith direct from the holy.

. . . The major element in the creation is to know that the world was created and that God created the world by His will. This knowledge is founded on faith, because only faith can lead to a belief in the creation. The way of reason does not lead to an understanding of the creation, and that is why heretics and atheists deny that the world was created. We believe in God who created the world because we know that the creation really took place by means of an act of faith, as is shown by the verse that says: "and all His work is done in faithfulness" (Psalms 33:4). Thus, faith is the basic element of the creation, and the world was incomplete until the Torah was given, for through the Torah, by the power of the prophetic spirit, the people of Israel gained complete faith, as was explained above. This explains why the creation was revealed at that time— because it is dependent on faith.

The future renewal of the world[11] will also take place by the power of faith. We know this from the verse "For I have said, forever is mercy built" (Psalms 89:3),[12] which shows that the power of faith will bring about the assembling of the merciful powers that will cause the world's renewal.

. . . When the world is renewed in the future, it will be ruled by the power of miracles—that is, by divine providence alone, which is an aspect of miracles, and not by natural laws, for the future renewal of the world is an aspect of Eretz Yisrael.

(Source: *Likutey Moharan* II, chap. 8, sec. 8–10)

1. In Hasidic terminology, *le-hitkarev* ("to draw close") denotes the establishment of a close connection between a Hasid and his Zaddik.

2. "An aspect of" (*behinat*) is a kabbalistic term denoting that a certain lowly power is derived from a divine power; the relationship between the divine, hidden power and the revealed one is often symbolic—that is, the earthly phenomenon is a slight revelation of the hidden truth.

3. The term is derived from Numbers 14:24: "But My servant Caleb, because he had another spirit with him and hath followed Me fully."

4. The term is derived from Numbers 27:18: "And the Lord said unto Moses: Take thee Joshua the son of Nun, a man in whom is spirit."

5. "Derives" (*nimshach*) is a kabbalistic term which actually means "emanated"; here the author stresses that this spirit is emanated from the divine world, and not from the evil powers.

6. The author uses the verb *taken*, "to mend," a basic Lurianic term—to mend the broken aspects of the divine world (see Introduction).

7. The imagination is the region of the human soul in which the evil powers can emplace themselves and from there rule the person. Purification of the imagination means the sanctification of the whole soul.

8. Based on I Kings 22:23: "Now therefore, behold, the Lord hath put a lying spirit in the mouth of all these thy prophets."

9. The "venom" or "dirt" of the snake is a symbol of the first mixing of good and evil in Adam and Eve.

10. Based on B. Shabbat 146a.

11. The term that Rabbi Nahman uses here, *hidush ha-olam*, can mean both "creation" and "renewal."

12. Literally: "the world will be built by charity."

REGULATIONS CONCERNING VISITS TO THE ZADDIK

A Letter by Rabbi Shneur Zalman, 1793.

Greetings of peace and life without end. I have an urgent request for all my friends and those who love me, and for all those who belong to us,[1] especially those who are charged with supervising religious matters, the officers of the appeal for the Holy Land, may it be built soon, Amen. Please take great care, as if it were a matter of life and death, to stop God's people who are traveling to our place and warn them, upon their souls, not to cause me grief by coming here at the wrong time (further on I will explain what I mean by this). Speak with all the pilgrims, whether they are from your towns or from other towns or just passing through; show them a copy of this letter and strictly warn them that each of the following regulations is based on truth and justice and must not be transgressed.

First of all, those who intend to visit on the four known occasions[2] will not be permitted to enter my house and speak to me alone even on questions pertaining to the worship of God, much less on worldly matters, however important. It is simply impossible for me to meet personally with everyone who assembles here on the four known occasions. Furthermore, I cannot pick and choose among them. A jealousy as cruel as the grave (Song of Songs 8:6) is rampant among those who try to force their way into my house, and because I am so soft-hearted, I would not be able to endure the sorrow of those who went home dissatisfied and jealous because they were not selected. It angers and embitters me, and makes me fear God's judgment, to reject anyone who wants to approach God's worship and desperately needs to consult me alone, especially new followers, but what else can I do? Time does not permit private conversations with each of the new people who congregate here on the four occasions, and I cannot make distinctions among them, accepting some and rejecting others. Therefore, new followers who come here on the four occasions should not expect to meet with me privately. If they want to consult me, they should not come here on the four occasions. Instead they should come on one of the first three Sabbaths of whatever month they prefer and should stay here for two or three days after the Sabbath.

However, on the fourth Sabbath, when the new month is blessed, new followers may not come here. This Sabbath is reserved for our old followers, to ensure them at least one opportunity a year to consult me, as used to be our practice. After the fourth Sabbath I will have no time to meet privately with new followers because I will be occupied with the old, and even this only in regard to important matters on which our people in their own towns cannot advise them. This permission to meet privately with me is strictly conditional. An old follower can consult me only if he is faced with two

alternatives and cannot choose between them. However, if a follower knows he has only one option, but is reluctant because it is
degrading, heaven forbid, and he wants to discuss his fears with me,
then he must write to me or inform my secretary.[3] Rest assured that
I will be informed of everything he says, with nothing omitted, and
if I have anything to say to him, he will receive my answer in the
same manner. But he must not force his way into my house.

I can no longer endure the sorrow and bitterness caused by
those who come here to tell me all their troubles and make me share
their sorrow. I can no longer endure even those who come to ask my
advice on matters that are not tragic and do not concern trouble. I
can no longer endure all the confusion and the interference with my
worship of God, and in any case, the profusion of troubles and
problems among our many followers, may God increase your numbers a thousandfold and give you His blessing of peace so that you
can remain home in peace, makes it impossible for me to consider
problems in the depth required if I am to provide correct answers.

(Source: *Igrot Ba'al Ha-Tania*, chap. 39)

1. *Anshey shelomenu*, a term used in Habad to denote members of the sect. It
occurs frequently in this and similar documents.

2. The four times in the year when most Hasidim visit the Zaddik: the festival of
Simhat Torah, the Sabbath of Hanukkah, Purim, and the Sabbath between Rosh
Hashanah and Yom Kippur.

3. *Ne'eman beiti*, the officer in charge of the Zaddik's home and personal affairs.

THE ASCENSION OF THE BESHT'S SOUL

On Rosh Hashanah in the year 507[1] I used divine names to bring
about the ascension of my soul, as you know, and in my vision I saw
wondrous things—things I had never seen before. It is impossible to
describe the things I saw and learned during my ascension or to
discuss them with anyone else, but when I returned to Lower
Paradise[2] I saw the souls of some who are dead and some who are
alive, some whom I know and some whom I do not know, countless
in number, moving up and down[3] in their attempt to ascend from
world to world by means of the pillar[4] that is known to scholars of
the Kabbalah. They were rejoicing in a great happiness that no

human mouth can describe and no mortal ear can hear. Many sinners returned and repented, and their sins were forgiven because it was a time of divine good will. I was surprised that the repentance of some of them was accepted—you know whom I mean. They were all rejoicing greatly as they participated in these ascensions.

All of them together addressed me at great length. "Your honor," they implored, "because of your standing in Torah, God has given you a special intelligence that enables you to understand and know these things. Please ascend with us and give us your help and support." Because of their great happiness, I was about to ascend with them.

Then in a vision I saw Satan ascending to act as prosecutor, and he was unspeakably happy as he performed his work of persecution, causing several people to be killed with horrible tortures. I was overcome by terror, and at the risk of endangering my own soul I asked my rabbi and teacher[5] to accompany me because ascending to the higher world is so dangerous. From the day I began such practices I have never ascended so high. I ascended from one stage to another until I entered the palace of the Messiah. In that place, where the Messiah studies Torah with the Tannaim,[6] the Zaddikim, and the seven shepherds,[7] I witnessed great rejoicing. I could not understand why they were so happy and assumed it was because I had died and departed from the earthly world, heaven forbid. Later they told me that I was not dead, thanks to their enjoyment of the *yihudim*[8] which I do down here on earth, assisted by their holy scholarship, but to this day I do not know the real reason for the joy I witnessed.

Then I asked the Messiah when he would come. He replied, "When your teachings have been revealed in the world and become famous, when the springs of your teachings have spread everywhere, including what I have taught you, and when others are able to do *yihudim* and ascensions as you do—then all the evil powers will perish, and then it will be a time of divine good will and the time of redemption." I was very surprised and was sad about the length of time,[9] for when could all this really happen?

But while I was there I learned three things of medicine[10] and three sacred holy names, which were easy to learn and explain. This encouraged me, because I felt that with their help the people of my era would be able to achieve the same status I had achieved—that is, that they would be able to ascend their souls and achieve the same knowledge and understanding that I have achieved. But I was not granted permission to reveal this knowledge during my life. I asked for permission to reveal it to you but did not receive it, and I am still sworn to secrecy on this matter.

(Source: *The Besht's Epistle, Ben Porat Yosef,* Appendix)

1. In this letter, which was written about 1750, the Besht described a vision he had seen three years earlier. The letter was written to Rabbi Gershon of Kitov, his brother-in-law (see Sources).

2. The vision itself took place in a higher region of the divine world; now he descended to a lower region (see note 4).

3. *Razo va-shov,* denoting the dynamic movement in the divine world; the term is taken from Ezekiel 1:14: "And the living creatures *ran and returned* as the appearance of a flash of lightning."

4. Probably a reference to the ninth sefirah, Yesod, which is the central pillar in the lower sefirot in kabbalistic terminology.

5. A reference to the prophet Ahijah the Shilonite, the teacher of the prophet Elijah; according to Hasidic tradition, especially in the works of Rabbi Ya'akov Yosef of Polonnoye, he was the Besht's rabbi.

6. The early sages, the authors of the Mishnah.

7. The patriarchs: Abraham, Isaac, Jacob, Joseph, Moses, Aaron, and David.

8. *Yihud* means bringing the separated divine powers together by praying with intention and by semi-magical techniques, using holy names and theurgical practices.

9. Obviously the Besht did not believe that any such thing was likely to occur in his lifetime or the near future.

10. *Segulot,* usually a reference to magical means of healing either body or soul.

RABBI NAHMAN'S SELF-PITY

Around the time of the festival of Shavuot in the year 565 (= 1805) I went to see him [Rabbi Nahman] with my friend Rabbi Naphtali. He told us that he knew nothing, except that the evil tongues in the world were making it impossible for the Zaddikim to achieve the state of humbleness,[1] as is explained in paragraph 197 of the homily.[2] Aside from this, he said, he knew nothing at all. His words were quite explicit: "Like you, I really do not know anything."[3] His daily routine, he told us, was quite simple. He got up in the morning to pray, said the prayer, and then studied a little and recited some Psalms; after eating he would sleep for a while, then get up and speak to God, asking for mercy and pleading with God; and then, he said, "I have pity on myself."[3] He said these words with such great earnestness and contrition that anyone who heard him understood that he pitied himself with an intensity that would have been appropriate if he had been as distant from God as it is possible to be, heaven forbid.

During the same visit he related one of his dreams to us. In the dream it was Shavuot, and all of his disciples had gathered around him for the festival. But he was unable to teach or to say a homily and instead abused and admonished us, saying that our attachment to material things made it impossible for him to say the homily. (As we all know, the Zaddik's wisdom derives from the people who gather around him.) So he admonished us without letup, and because of this we all repented and were roused to deep regret and repentance.

Later he said a wonderful and mysterious homily.

(Source: *Hayey Moharan* I, 24)

1. This is a reference to the renewal of antagonism toward Rabbi Nahman at that time. The idea is that a Zaddik should be too humble to praise himself, but his critics made this impossible.

2. *Likutey Moharan Kama*. Humbleness, it is explained there, results from wisdom; without wisdom it is impossible, and as Rabbi Nahman was then in a state of ignorance, he could not be humble.

3. The writer, Rabbi Nathan, quotes this sentence both in his Hebrew translation and in the Yiddish original, for emphasis.

RABBI NAHMAN AND RABBI NATHAN

Throughout our lives we must offer thanks and praise to the Maker of the great lights, whose blessings last forever, and who made the sun, our master and teacher Rabbi Nahman, to rule during the day, because our blessed Zaddik, may his memory be blessed, is like the sun in the power of his light and shining glory, which shines during the day. There is hidden significance in this, for it denotes the redemption, when his hidden book and his burned book will be revealed,[1] as well as the great, enormous secrets in his esoteric teachings which we already know.[2] And He gave the moon to rule at night.[3] This is his disciple, our teacher Rabbi Nathan, may his memory be blessed, who is like the moon because he purified his body until he was able to receive the light of the sun and make it shine even in the darkness of our generation.[4] In this way he gave life and showed the way of repentance to all those people of limited vision who were unable to look at the light of the sun itself because of the weakness of their eyes.

(Source: From the introduction by Rabbi Abraham, son of Rabbi Nahman of Tolchin, to the collection *Kochvei Or*, p. *v.*)

1. According to the traditions of the Bratslav sect, Rabbi Nahman of Bratslav burned one of his books and hid another.

2. It was a principal belief of all kabbalists, and still is, that the Torah's esoteric secrets will be revealed in the time of the redemption. Many kabbalists held that the beginning of the age of redemption had been heralded by either the revelation, the printing, or the true interpretation of the Zohar. Here Rabbi Abraham transfers this belief to the teachings of Rabbi Nahman, maintaining that in the time of the redemption Rabbi Nahman's unknown works will be revealed and the true meaning of his extant works will become known.

3. In kabbalistic symbolism, the sun and the the moon represent the sixth and tenth sefirot (Tiferet and Malchut). A special section of *Kochvei Or*, however, is dedicated to linking Rabbi Nahman with a higher sefirah, Binah (the third).

4. This is a reference to Rabbi Nathan's written works. Rabbi Nahman did not himself put his teachings into written form, but Rabbi Nathan preserved them for later generations.

PART THREE

THE RELIGIOUS
LIFE

IN SEARCH OF THE HIDDEN GOD

God's hiding has two degrees: His hiding behind one cover, and His hiding behind a cover that is beyond the first cover. It is very difficult to find God when He is hidden behind one cover, but not impossible if the searcher tries hard enough, because at least he knows from the outset that God is hidden from him. When God is hidden behind the cover that is beyond the first cover, however, the fact of His being hidden is unknown to the searcher, and without this knowledge it is impossible to find Him.

Anyone who repeatedly trangresses and sins falls into the shadow of the cover behind which God is hiding. It is very difficult to extricate oneself from this predicament by repenting and return-ing, because God is hidden, and in consequence, at least so it seems, sins are permitted. The person in this predicament is not devoid of knowledge, however; he still knows that God is hidden from him, and he knows that it seems to him that sinful acts are permitted. As a result, he may still have an awareness, in his heart of hearts, of having fallen so low that God and Torah are hidden and sins seem permitted; this awareness may motivate him to try to extricate himself from this predicament.

But if, heaven forbid, he doesn't simply sin once or twice but continues on his evil path, performing deeds that become progres-sively more wicked, he falls into the cover beyond the first cover, and then God and Torah are hidden from him to such an extent that he does not know that the things he is doing are prohibited. He does not even have the distorted belief that the sinful things he is doing are permitted even though sinful, for in his mind wicked deeds seem to be a right and completely honest pattern of behavior, as if there were no laws at all.

Even then one should not despair, however, for we should not despair about anything in this world. Even if one has fallen to such a lowly state that God is hidden from him in the cover beyond the first cover, the divine life which originated in God is still present, though in a disguised form, because without this divine life nothing in the world could exist. The satanic forces themselves and the great sins—even the places that are hidden by the cover beyond the first cover—still receive life from God. Whoever is fortunate enough to know these facts will merit the removal of all the covers so that he can hear the voice of the divine crier of the Torah, the voice that constantly shouts, "How long, ye thoughtless, will ye love thoughtlessness?" (Proverbs 1:122), and one who hears the voice will merit returning to God.

The merit of knowing all this is achieved through Torah. Studying the Torah can even awaken someone for whom God is hidden in the cover beyond the first cover, informing him, from God, that his situation is not hopeless and he may yet return to the truth and draw near to God by repenting.

No matter what a seeker's state of life may be, it is always possible for him to draw near to God through the power of the true Zaddikim. Even if one has done wicked things and fallen to wherever he had to fall, heaven forbid, the divine life is still present for him in disguise, because it gives life to everything. Thus, one can return from any place and may merit hearing the voice of the Torah, as was explained above. Because of the many covers behind which God is hidden due to the multiplicity of sins, we do not always hear the voice of the great crier of the Torah, and God is eclipsed from us in a cover beyond a cover, in the aspect of "And I will surely hide My face in that day" (Deuteronomy 31:18).[1] But Torah study can remove the covers, so that even those who are very far away can hear the voice of the crier of the Torah, and all can repent and return to God.

(Source: *Kitzur Likutey Moharan* 56, sec. 5)

1. The point of the quotation is lost in the translation. In the Hebrew the verse begins with two forms of the verb "to hide" (*haster astir*), as a means of expressing emphasis ("I will *surely* hide . . ."), and this double use of the verb is the basis for Rabbi Nahman's conclusion that the verse refers to the doubly-hidden God.

THE PURPOSE OF WORSHIP

Worship and business have similar purposes. You do business for only one reason—to make a profit. Worship is also intended to make a profit—to uplift the divine sparks that fell during the breaking of the vessels[1] and were clothed in material things: animal, vegetable, mineral, and human. Man's worship through Torah and commandments uplifts these sparks, so that they are transformed from darkness to light and ascend higher and higher among the divine lights. Each of us, in accordance with the merits of his worship, profits from participating in this process.

The foregoing pertains to the worship of those who are completely righteous and have never sinned. The real purpose of worhsip, however, pertains to the aspect of the penitent[2]—the worship of God from the aspect of the supreme fear, the fear of shame, risking one's soul and negating existence. Our sages of blessed memory were alluding to this when they said that not everyone who does business on a large scale becomes wise (Avot 2:5), meaning that worship should not only be for profit but should also be from the aspect of the penitent—supreme fear, risking of the soul, and negation of existence. One should not be preoccupied with his own actions and feelings while praying—worship should take place in complete negation and abolition of awareness of the self.

(Source: *Kedushat Levi, Likutim*)

1. See Introduction.
2. See below, p. 122–124, "The Pentitent" (translated from the same passage of *Kedushat Levi*).

FREE CHOICE

A famous saying of our sages[1] teaches us that a lit candle hovers over the head of a baby in its mother's womb, and by its light he can see from one end of the world to the other. In other words, the baby still possesses the holiness that was his before he left his original place in the divine world. At the moment of birth, however, so the saying tells us, an angel slaps the baby on the mouth, causing him to forget everything he knew until then.

When the time comes for the baby to enter the world, he is enveloped by an outpouring of holy, divine light from above so that he can concentrate all his thoughts on the uninterrupted worship of God. But since God wills that that we humans should have the ability to sacrifice ourselves body and soul to his worship, he cuts off the outpouring of divine light. It remains thereafter only as a partition between the newborn and the world, and God gives the baby the ability to choose between good and evil.

Those who are able to think clearly realize that this world is completely evil and that all worldly pleasures are transient since everything that lives is in the process of dying and decay is the fate of all flesh. They understand that the only real good in this world is the worship of God, which can sustain them forever. Anyone who understands this will never forsake good and choose evil. Instead, he will commit himself to the worship of God, and if he does so, he may be able to regain his original status in the divine world. Since his material body will become more spiritual and will no longer have the same character it had when he was born, the partition between himself and the divine light will be shattered, permitting him to break through; when he does, he will be overcome by a great enlightenment from the light referred to in the verse that says, "the light of the king's countenance is life" (Proverbs 16:15)—an enlightenment as brilliant as the rising of the sun.

(Source: *Kedushat Levi: Va-Yeshev*)

1. What follows is an interpretation of the rabbinic saying in B. Niddah 30b.

PRAYER AND COMMUNION (I)

In order to preserve your strength and not use it all up at the beginning of your prayer, ascend toward communion with God in stages. Hold yourself back at the outset so that you can achieve an intense degree of communion in the middle, and then recite the remaining words of the prayer quickly, as if running.

When you are beginning to pray, if you feel that you will not be able to achieve a state of communion, concentrate intensely as you recite the words and gradually fortify yourself; and God will help you to achieve the state of prayer with a high degree of communion.

Train yourself to whisper in prayer even while reciting the Psalms. Learn to shout in a low voice, and enunciate every part of the prayers, even the selections from the Psalms and the Torah, with all your might, in the sense indicated by the verse: "All my bones shall say" (Psalms 35:10). The shout that results from communion should be uttered in a whisper.

(Source: *Zava'at Ha-Rivash*)

PRAYER AND COMMUNION (II)

Every letter in the prayer is a complete world in itself,[1] and if you do not recite the prayer with all your strength, so that this aspect of it is realized, the prayer will be incomplete, as if one of its limbs were missing.

It is only by God's grace that we remain alive after praying, because in the normal course of events, death would result from the tremendous exertion required to implement the prayer's requisite intentionality.[2]

Sometimes you can recite the words of the prayer very quickly, because the love of God is burning so strongly in your heart that the words seem to flow from your mouth by themselves in a whisper.

When you achieve communion with the divine world, you will have attained such merit that the divine powers will raise you even higher during your prayer, for as our sages of blessed memory said, "He who comes in order to be purified will be helped" (see B. Shabbat 104a, B. Yoma 38b). The power of your prayer will enable you to achieve the merit of uniting your thought[3] with the divine world, and this will give you the power to reach an even higher degree, so that you can be in a state of communion with the divine world even when you are not praying.

Do not weaken yourself by reciting too many Psalms before praying. If you do, you will not have enough strength left to recite the really important prayers with great communion—the mandatory prayers, such as the hymns, the Shema, and the benedictions. Begin by reciting the mandatory prayer with intense communion. Then, if God gives you enough strength, recite the Psalms and the Song of Songs with intense communion.

On Yom Kippur, before the concluding prayer, the *ne'ilah*, recite the prayers in a lowly manner[4] so that afterward you will be able to pray with communion.[5]

When you are in a state of lowliness, it is preferable to use a prayerbook when praying, because you will be able to pray with more concentration and intention if you have the text of the prayers before you. But when you are in a state of communion with the divine world, it is better to close your eyes, so that seeing does not prevent you from uniting yourself with the divine world.

The soul told our rabbi that he merited the revelation of divine things not because he had learned so much Talmud and halakhah, but because he always prayed with a high degree of intentionality.[6]

(Source: *Zava'at Ha-Rivash*)

1. *Komah shlemah*, meaning a complete *shiur komah*—in kabbalistic symbolism, the divine body, including all the sefirot. Every letter in the prayers contains symbolic elements representing the complete structure of the divine world.

2. *Kavvanot*, the spiritual intentions that are to be included in the prayer. The code of these intentions was perfected by Isaac Luria, though various Hasidic teachers reacted differently to it.

3. A literal translation, but here *mahshavah* means the spiritual part of man, the part that can ascend to the divine world.

4. *Be-katnut*, "in smallness," opposed to *gadlut*, "greatness," which here means *devekut*, "communion."

5. That is, one should restrain himself while reciting the nonessential prayers, preserving his power for the *ne'ilah*, the most important prayer.

6. This is a reference to the practice of *aliyat neshamah* ("ascension of the soul") by the Besht ("our rabbi"). The Besht would spiritually ascend his soul to the divine world, and when it returned, it would reveal to him what it had seen there. This practice is mentioned in the writings of Rabbi Ya'akov Yosef and in the *Shivhey ha-Besht*, as well as in the Besht's letter to his brother-in-law (printed in Rabbi Ya'akov Yosef's *Ben Porat Yosef* [Koretz, 1781]; see "The Ascension of the Besht's Soul," above, pp. 96–98.

INTENTIONALITY IN WORSHIP

When you begin to pray, your *kavvanah*[1] should be so concentrated that you are ready to die during the prayer. Some people, in fact, achieve such an intense state of *kavvanah* while praying to God that in ordinary circumstances they would die after reciting only two or three words. In light of this, you should say to yourself: "Since so and so is prepared to die after only two or three words, why should my prayer be marred by pride or some other defect?" Indeed, it is only God's great charity that gives a person the strength to complete his prayer and remain alive.

When you fast, your intention should be: "Alas, my desires and false pride have angered the supreme king, and therefore I wish to mortify myself and overcome my desire and pride, fulfilling the commandment of repentance and thereby causing my master in the divine world to overcome his slave and the mistress, her servant.[2] I wish to mortify myself in order to worship God with all my heart, in love and fear of God, in order to bring about His unity by my efforts.[3] By fasting I offer myself to Him a sacrificial lamb.

"Alas, what am I, what is my life? I want to sacrifice my blood and my fat, my body, my spirit, my soul, my strength, my heart, and my arms to Him, to the creator of all the worlds, to Him by whose words all the worlds were made and before whom everything that exists is like nothing. I who am but earth and worms cannot ask anything of Him but His great charity in giving me the strength to offer many sacrifices before Him.

"I should rejoice at the fact that my body, my spirit, and my soul have caused God some pleasure. I should also rejoice at the fact that God has given us a means by which we can overcome our evil desires.

"I want to fast because I have caused sorrow to God and His Shekhinah, and I also want to fast to remove the Shekhinah's sorrow.

"Alas, what good is my mortification, since for so many years I have caused God to sorrow? I have no right to ask God for anything and can only appeal to His great charity to observe the self-mortification I am undertaking in order to remove sorrow from His Shekhinah, and to remove the evil powers from us.

"In this way I can cause the evil powers in the divine world to leave the Shekhinah, so that she can be purified and completely reunited with her husband in a union of charity and mercy. The power of my mortification will also bring about a union between the divine world and the lower worlds, and the divine emanation will descend from stage to stage[4] until it reaches me.

"I trust completely in Him who created all the worlds *ex nihilo* by the power of his words, He who is incomparable and takes care of all the worlds, giving them the divine emanation and their vitality. Surely He can also provide me with strength from above and can care for me through his charity, saving me from my evil desires so that they will not prevent me from fulfilling my intention of mortifying myself. The evil desire may tell me that I am weak and my mind is withering, and may put me through other trials. That is why I am appealing to His great charity to give me strength, for He it was who enabled my heart to decide to do this and helped me many times before by His charity. May He help me and save me today too, from anything that might prevent me from doing as I intend.

"I must not regard my mortification as something that comes on my own, for I am nothing and everything emanates from God. On my own I would be completely unable to mortify myself.

"I am giving myself completely to Him who created all the worlds by speaking, even if I must suffer mortifications and slanders of every kind for the sake of His unity. I wish to achieve what is stated in the verse that says: "Sanctify yourselves therefore, and be ye holy" (Leviticus 20:7), and I have trust that God's great charity will supply me with the extra strength I need to worship Him truly.

"God will help me so that people will not know what I am doing. I am not afraid of the weakness that may result from my fasting, because many people become ill even if they do not fast. Furthermore, the Shekhinah takes care of the sick (B. Shabbat 12b), as shown by 'The Lord supporteth him upon the bed of illness' (Psalms 41:4). He will support me with His charity too."

(Source: *Zava'at Ha-Rivash*)

1. The spiritual intentionality that accompanies the performance of every commandment.

2. If someone in this world overcomes the evil within him, then in the divine world, symbolically, the divine powers overcome Satan and the evil powers (here called "slave" and "servant").

3. The influence of the evil powers in the divine world causes the separation between God and the Shekhinah. When these powers are weakened, God and the Shekhinah draw close to each other and true unity in the divine world is achieved. The "unity of God" is not a constant state, but a desired state toward which man's religious efforts are directed.

4. The physical symbolism of "from mind to heart, from heart to liver" demonstrates the descent of the divine emanation (*shefa*).

UNION IN PRAYER

Prayer is a coupling[1] with the Shekhinah. Like a physical coupling, it should begin with movements. Move your body when you start your prayer, then stand still and enjoy the profound communion with the Shekhinah. Moving your body in worship, thus reminding yourself that the Shekhinah is standing before you, will rouse you to a state of intense excitement.

(Source: *Zava'at Ha-Rivash*)
1. *Zivug*, sexual union.

TRIAL IN PRAYER

When you start to pray and begin with the preparatory verse "O Lord, open Thou my lips" (Psalms 51:17), the Shekhinah enters you[1] and recites the words of the prayer.[2] If you are aware that it is the Shekhinah that is reciting the words of the prayer, you will be overcome by fear of God, and then God will concentrate Himself and enter you,[3] in the sense conveyed by the verse that says, "He peereth through the lattice" (Song of Songs 2:9). The letters of the prayers represent the divine palaces; you will go from palace to palace, and at each palace you will be tested to see whether you are worthy of entering. If we all understood that we are on trial whenever we have an evil thought, undoubtedly we would always pray with the right intention—but we forget that we are on trial.

(Source: *Maggid Devarav Le Ya'akov*, chap. 2)

1. *Mitlabeshet bo*, "is incarnated in him."

2. According to the Maggid, a person who achieves *devekut*, cannot pray, and it is the Shekhinah who prays from within him.

3. The Maggid uses the term *zimzum* for God's contact with the person who is praying (see Introduction).

THE HIDDEN KING

You must not give in to the occasional feeling that you cannot pray; instead, fortify yourself by strengthening your fear of God. To understand why you should do this, bear in mind the story of the king who once tried to hide from his enemies during a war by dressing in a commoner's clothing. Those who were wise recognized him anyway because his mannerisms were familiar; but even those who were not wise were able to recognize him because it was so obvious that only a king would be surrounded by so many guards and attendants. So it is when you cannot pray with the proper degree of intentionality.

In order to focus your thoughts, remind yourself that the very "guards" who are preventing you from getting through prove that the king is really there. By strengthening yourself with fear of God and heightening your concentration, you will be able to break through the "guards" and draw close to Him, and then you will be able to pray with the appropriate degree of intentionality.

(Source: *Zava'at Ha-Rivash*)

THE UPLIFTING OF EVIL THOUGHTS

Although you probably already understand and uphold the following rule, I will explain it anyway because our sainted teacher, Rabbi Dov Baer of blessed memory, wrote books about it that were read by many people, although few at the time were able to emulate him, even to the slightest degree, in either manner or deed. Rabbi Dov Baer said that a person in whom a forbidden love is kindled thinks that he can unite it with love for the Creator, reasoning[1] that if he loves something unworthy, something which is no more than the rubbish that fell during the breaking of the vessels,[2] then he can certainly desire and love the divine source from whence it originally came, and this is the love of the Creator. And the same reasoning is applied to bad fear,[3] bad pride and arguments, and so forth.

If they are not wise, the people who reason this way may think that it is as easy to make a substitution of this kind as it is to make certain similar substitutions in the Talmud. But the substitutions in the Talmud pertain only to studying, whereas here it is a matter of doing. Thus their reasoning is false, unless the person working the substitution could be completely removed from his material body. For if he is united with matter and desires, and can derive pleasure from them at will, he certainly knows nothing at all about his own pride or about loving and fearing the Creator, because he has never tasted it, in the sense indicated by the verse that says: "O consider and see[4] that the Lord is good" (Psalms 34:9).

A person who does this will fall into a deep abyss,[5] heaven forbid, unless he is very cautious and protects himself. He should keep himself away from evil desires, using all the methods discussed in the books on ethics. Rabbi Dov Baer's advice about how to bring the precious out of the cheap by making this substitution is only relevant for someone who is completely separated from the material world, although an occasional thought of evil love or evil fear may still enter his heart because he is not yet completely purified and the evil powers are trying to push him toward evil. By working this substitution, such a person can make his love for the Creator, and his fear of God, burn with new force.[6]

(Source: *Yosher Divrey Emet*, chap. 16)

1. The author uses the term *kal va-homer* ("light and heavy"), a talmudic term for the process of making an inference from one premise with the help of another, when the known premise is obviously more important than the unknown one (i.e., reasoning "from major to minor").

2. The Lurianic concept according to which the evil things in this world are the product of the pre-creation catastrophe in the divine world. The root of every evil thing is, therefore, divine, and was originally a part of the divine entity.

3. "Bad fear" in this context is usually forbidden anger.

4. In Hebrew, literally: "O taste and see."

5. A reference to hell.

6. This blunt criticism of a practice so frequently described in the writings of Rabbi Dov Baer and in *Zava'at Ha-Rivash* is unusual, though most Hasidic teachers accepted Rabbi Meshulam's view and decided that the practice was only appropriate for a Zaddik.

EVIL THOUGHTS (I)

If someone succeeds in overcoming the evil thoughts that enter his mind, God is very pleased and regards him as precious. It is very much like what happens when a king celebrates a festival by staging a fight between wild beasts because he enjoys seeing one beast defeat another. Thoughts emanate from the aspect of the divine creatures described in Ezekiel's vision of the chariot (Ezekiel 1), sacred thoughts from the aspect of the pure creatures, and evil thoughts to fight each other, and He is happy when a human being defeats one of the impure creatures.

Since the human mind cannot think about two things at once, it is easy to drive evil thoughts away. The process is passive rather than active: simply think about something else, such as Torah or the worship of God or even your everyday affairs. It is not necessary to fight the evil thought actively or to move your head from side to side in an effort to drive it away; none of this helps, and fixing your attention on the evil thought may even strengthen it. The only thing that works is to ignore the evil thought and concentrate fully on whatever you are doing, whether studying the Torah or praying or working. Do not turn around. If you heed this advice, the evil thoughts will go away of their own accord.

(Source: *Likutey Moharan* I, chap. 233)

EVIL THOUGHTS (II)

Whenever you are tempted to commit a sin, read aloud the biblical verses that pertain to it, taking care to vocalize and chant all the words correctly. If you are animated by love and fear of God while doing this, the sinful desire will leave you.

If you are in danger of developing a sinful trait,[1] heaven forbid, recite out loud the names of the seven peoples—Canaanites, Hittites, etc. (Deuteronomy 7:1, etc.)—six times, with all your might, and with love and fear of God, and the danger will leave you.

You must establish a connection between your sinful desire and God. For example, if you are tempted to a sinful form of love, direct all your love at God alone, concentrating your every effort on this. If you are feeling anger, which is a sinful form of fear, emanating from the power of Gevurah,[2] overcome this desire by transforming it into a chariot supporting the divine world.

If you hear a preacher speaking about God with great love and fear, unite yourself with the preacher's words and become one with him. The preacher's words will then become thoughts in your mind, and this will cause any evil thoughts to leave you.[3]

(Source: *Zava'at Ha-Rivash*)

1. *Midah ra'ah*, as opposed to sin, is usually a deep moral flaw rather than a temporary wish to stray from one of the precepts.

2. In kabbalistic symbolism, the fifth sefirah—the source of divine justice and punishment, and therefore the source of both divine anger and sinful anger.

3. This short homily suggests five different ways of overcoming evil thoughts, but whereas the first two and the last are aimed at driving the thoughts away, the middle ones direct the reader to retain his desire and transform it into a constructive spiritual force. This ideological mixture is typical of the earliest Hasidic works; the distinction between the two different attitudes later became clear, and Hasidic teachers developed various formulas concerning each of them.

COMMUNION AND STUDY (I)

If you are still sleepy when you get up at midnight to study, drive away your drowsiness by chanting hymns and pacing back and forth.

Study several different subjects, because one subject can become tiresome.

When you study, pause for a while every hour to establish communion with God.

While it is impossible for someone who is studying to establish communion with God, studying is still necessary. Torah study brightens the soul, because the Torah is "a tree of life to them that lay hold upon her" (Proverbs 3:18). If you do not study, your communion will fail.

Bear in mind that since you cannot establish communion while sleeping or while your mind is in a state of lowliness,[1] nothing is lost by studying.[2] In any case, practice communion with God whenever it is possible.

(Source: *Zava-ut Ha-Rivash*)

1. Literally: "when his minds fall," i.e., when he is in a state of *katnut* ("smallness").

2. The attitude toward Torah study here, equating it with sleeping or light-mindedness, infuriated the opponents of Hasidism, and they used this text in their campaign against the movement.

COMMUNION AND STUDY (II)

If you are studying the Torah and break off to talk to someone, keep your mind on communion with God. But when you are studying keep your mind on the subject being studied, and if you do so, you will receive proper communion with God later on.

It is necessary to study the Torah every once in a while because the Torah is "a tree of life to them that lay hold upon her" (Proverbs 3:18). But when you are talking about things of no consequence, you should be in a state of communion with God.

Take care not to become so preoccupied with your daily Torah study that you fall from the state of communion with God.[1] If you are careful, then later on, if you have a problem deciding whether to do something, you will be able to find the answer using the Torah you have learned that day. If you are always in a state of communion with God, then God will make sure that the questions confronting you can be answered by the Torah you have studied. But if your behavior toward God is dishonest, God will treat you with casual disinterest.[2] Moreover, He will not uplift you by providing clothes and food containing sparks from the source of your soul.[3]

(Source: Zava'at Ha-Rivash)

1. In other words, studying or thinking about halakhic problems requires so much spiritual and intellectual concentration that it prevents the establishment of a state of communion. All other occupations, however, leave the mind and soul free to practice communion. Therefore when someone starts to think about what he has studied, he is in great danger of lapsing from the state of communion.

2. The text here has an untranslatable pun (be-keri, ba-akrai).

3. The human soul is derived from a certain place in the divine world. When the divine world underwent the catastrophe of the shevirah, sparks from all of its stages were scattered in the material world, some of them serving as the souls of the animals from which food and clothes are prepared. When a pious person eats or dresses properly (in the religious sense), he can uplift these sparks; if God favors someone, He will provide him with sparks that derive from the same place in the divine world as his own soul. Punishment, on the other hand, may be meted out by preventing a person from having the opportunity to uplift the sparks that have a special significance for his own soul.

THE FEAR OF GOD

"And now, Israel, what doth the Lord they God require of thee but to fear the Lord thy God" (Deuteronomy 10:12). "To fear the Lord thy God" means that your fear should be like God's fear. Human fears usually concern inconsequential things like punishment, but God's fear—the fear He casts over us—concerns sin. Because of His great compassion and love, God is constantly afraid, so to speak, that we may sin, much as a father is constantly afraid that his son may get sick or choose the wrong path. Thus: "And now, Israel, what doth the Lord thy God require of thee" means that your fear, like God's, should be fear of sin.

A comparison from everyday life will clarify this. A father once told his young son not to walk barefooted because he might step on a thorn. The boy ignored the father's warning and pricked his foot. Afraid that an infection might develop unless the thorn was removed, the father pried it out with a sharp needle, in the process ripping the surrounding flesh. Stepping on the thorn had not been painful, but removing it hurt so much that the boy began to cry. The father ignored the boy's weeping, however, because he knew it was unavoidable if the wound was to heal properly. Sometime later the boy again wanted to walk barefooted. The father reminded him of how much removing the thorn had hurt and warned that he would have to experience the same pain again if he persisted in walking barefoot. But he did not warn the child about the possibility of stepping on a thorn again. There would have been no point in doing this, because to the child's way of thinking, it was removing the thorn, and not stepping on the thorn, that had caused the pain. The father, of course, was really worried about the infection that might result if the boy stepped on a thorn again, but he mentioned the removal of the thorn because that is what the boy remembered and feared. The father, in other words, feared one thing; the boy, another; and thus we see that their fears were not one and the same.

The meaning of this story is self-evident. Human beings fear the punishment that results from sin rather than the sin itself; God fears the sin but not the punishment—indeed, since He punishes us only in order to purify us from our sins, He knows that the punishment is an act of divine mercy intended to heal the sinner. "And now, Israel, what doth the Lord thy God require of thee" calls this to our attention, urging that we, like God, fear the sin, not the punishment.

(Source: *Or Torah: Ekev*)

TWO TYPES OF FEAR OF GOD

Perfect fear of God entails two elements—superior fear and lower fear. Anyone who has true knowledge understands that it is impossible to perpetually remain at the highest religious level, as is shown by the secret meaning of "the living creatures ran and returned" (Ezekiel 1:14).[1] Because of this it is also necessary to have the lower fear, so that the fear of God is always within you, every day and in every way; enabling you to burn away evil thoughts even when you are not at the highest religious level and only possess the lower fear.

(Source: *Or Ha-Meir: Bereshit*)

1. This phrase from the description of the divine chariot was used consistently by Jewish mystics to denote the dynamic movements in the divine world, and later, as in Hasidism, the dynamic movement of the Zaddik or Hasid from stage to stage in the spiritual and earthly worlds.

WORSHIP IN FEAR

There are two kinds of human worship. The first is when someone is aware of the greatness of the Creator. He meditates on how God encircles and permeates all the worlds and is imcomparably superior to the worlds, the angels, and humanity. Through profound contemplation of God's greatness, he becomes a master of thought, understanding his own lowliness and the vast distance between himself and God. This enables him to achieve the aspect of supreme fear in obeying the Creator's commandments.

The second kind of human worship is the aspect of supreme fear. In this case one contemplates the aloofness of God's essence— the simple Ein Sof,[1] complete simplicity—and realizes that the human mind cannot understand anything about God. Someone who has this awareness is always in communion with the Creator's essence and in consequence achieves great fear and terror, as if all reality had completely ceased to exist. In this spirit he performs God's will by means of Torah and commandments and good deeds. His worship is not derived from contemplation of his own lowliness because he has no self-awareness whatsoever and is in a state of total negation. His worship derives from the nothingness of reality before the Creator's true essence.

The difference between the two kinds of worship can be illustrated by a parable about two servants of a king. One of the servants, motivated by a sense of his sovereign's magnificence and his own lowliness, serves the king faithfully even when he is faraway from the king; he obeys the king's commands even when they go against his own nature and preferences. The second servant serves the king faithfully because he is close to the king and understands his royal essence, negating his own existence so that he has no sense of himself at all. Since he has no sense of himself, he does not serve the king out of a feeling of lowliness compared to the king's greatness, and he does not humble or negate himself before the king; he feels the king's essence as the essence of his own self-awareness, and thus, in a state of complete personal negation before the king, carries out the king's will and performs his commands.

(Source: *Kedushat Levi, Likutim*)
1. See Introduction.

THE ORIGIN OF FEAR

Everything in the world is derived from the seven sefirot of structure.[1] Elements of all seven are contained in man, whose duty it is to uplift them to their source—God. For example, everyday fears emanate from divine fear, the lowest of the sefirot, also known as Shekhinah. If you experience an ordinary fear, you must ask yourself what you are really afraid of and where the fear comes from. Since the answer is that it comes from God's divine fear, you will realize, in the sense of "the whole earth is full of His glory" (Isaiah 6:3), that there is nothing to fear. Since there is nothing but God, and your own life is as nothing before Him, there is nothing to fear.

We must not fear anything but God's glory. When you achieve fear of God, you will understand that it is really a divine fear, deriving from a power that God created and containing emanations from God that make our existence possible. Since this fear derives its sustenance from an exalted divine source, it also contains love, albeit in a contracted way, for love is the emanation of life that makes existence possible. Knowing this will kindle your love for God, inspiring you with the enthusiasm of love.

(Source: *Pri Ez: Shoftim*)
1. The seven lower sefirot, from Hesed to Shekhinah, are the powers of creation.

LOVE OF GOD

Every member of the people of Israel has a share of the supreme God and can achieve understanding of the Creator's greatness, just as all of a man's sons are entitled to search for and share their father's hidden treasure. Through the process of observing and contemplating the Creator's greatness, one comes to see that God is the root and source of all the worlds: beyond and above them; circulating about them; indeed, so permeating them that there is no space from which He is absent. The awareness that all the worlds are as nothing before God, because nothing can stand before Him, fires the heart with love and desire for God, a passionate love that causes you to burn with the need to draw near to God and never be separated from Him—to be in constant communion with God, joined to Him always, in continued contact with His greatness and magnificence, not separated from Him even for the briefest of instants.

(Source: *Kedushat Levi, Likutim*)

REPENTANCE THROUGH LOVE

It says in the Gemara (B. Berakhot 32a) that the sins of a person who repents through love are transformed into merits. What happens to someone who repents out of love is the same as what happens to seeds that are sown in the earth—first they decay, and then plants emerge from them. That is why the same Gemara also says that repentance is so great that it ascends to the Throne of Glory. It means that the penitent himself ascends to the Throne of Glory and becomes a chariot to God.

(Source: *Degel Mahane Ephraim:* Haftarah of *Nizavim*)

HUMAN AND DIVINE LOVE

The blessed Creator has only one fear—that His love for us may cause us to sin. God wants to do good things for those He loves, because it is His way to do good for all His creatures, but He fears that those He loves may sin. Thus, the Creator's fear originates in love. Even the punishments He inflicts result from His desire to do good for His creatures, because punishment purifies us by suffering in this world so that we will be able to receive the good that awaits us in the next world, as is shown by the verse that says: "Thy wrath according to the fear that is due unto Thee" (Psalms 90:11). In other words, just as God's fear results from His love for man, so the wrath by which He punishes man also results from His love and is intended to benefit man in the end.

. . . Man should imitate God; just as God's fear is the outcome of love, so man's fear should be motivated by love for the Creator. Someone whose fear is motivated by love will always be afraid to sin, because he loves the Creator so much that he would never dare to commit a sin and thus, heaven forbid, cause a separation between himself and God.

The principle here is that you can only be afraid of something you can see,[1] and what you cannot see has nothing to do with fear. Love, however, pertains to the heart, and in your heart you can imagine anything, even something completely invisible. Since the blessed Creator is certainly invisible, even though He sees everything, you should focus the imaginings of your heart on envisioning His great power, His magnificence, and His miraculous nature, and in this way great love for God will enter your heart.

Furthermore, since thought originates in the Ein Sof, man can achieve great things with his power of thought, even imagining the infinite. Tie yourself with the ties of love. Through love you will achieve the fear of sin, for how could you dare commit a sin and thus separate yourself from this love, heaven forbid?

(Source: *Noam Elimelech: Vayigash*)

1. In Hebrew the words "fear" (*yir'ah*) and "seeing" (*re'iah*) are very similar, and Rabbi Elimelech concludes from this that fear is connected only with what is seen, but the invisible God ran be loved infinitely.

THE PENITENT

Our sages of blessed memory said that "in the place where penitents stand, the completely righteous cannot stand" (B. Sanhedrin 99a). This teaches us something about the nature of penitential worship. The saying refers not only to penitence after sinning but to people who have never sinned, for as our blessed sages also said, "A man should spend all his days in repentance" (B. Shabbat 153a), meaning that one should always be sorrowful about the distance between himself and God. If you constantly observe and contemplate the Creator's greatness, you will become of little value in your own eyes, and this will stimulate you to worship God with the supreme fear, the negation of your own existence. Then you will stretch yourself to reach God's presence.

Thus, "where penitents stand" means when you worship God through the aspect of repentance[1]—the aspect of supreme fear and the negation of your own existence. The completely righteous cannot stand where penitents stand, even though they are righteous and worship God through Torah and commandments and good deeds, because their hearts are not broken and filled with sorrow, and thus they cannot recognize their own lowliness by contemplating God's greatness, and they cannot cry out to Him from the depths of their hearts. One who cannot do this cannot ascend to the aspect of supreme fear and the negation of his own existence, and this, as we explained above, is the aspect of the penitent.

The talmudic saying with which we began this discussion also includes real penitents—people who have committed sins and incurred guilt before God; sinners who have drawn away from God, completely forgetting His ways and the steps by which one ascends to Him, making their hearts completely earthly, dumb, and material in the same sense indicated by the sages when they interpreted "Ye should be defiled thereby" (Leviticus 11:43) to mean that sin makes the heart dumb (Yoma 39a).[2] At first glance this is very strange. How can someone who has totally defiled and dirtied himself not only return to God but ascend higher than someone who was completely righteous and always worshiped God? This apparent mystery is cleared up by the following parable.

Once upon a time there was a servant who was always in the

king's court. All the other servants and guards respected him. He knew his way around the palace, was familiar with everything in it, and was continually in attendance on the king.

One day the servant rebelled against the king and fled to a far-off place. After a while he began to regret what he had done and fell into a deep sorrow. Finally he said to himself: "I know that the king is merciful. If I throw myself at his feet and beg him to forgive me, he will certainly forgive me. But how can I approach him? I no longer know my way around the palace, so I cannot simply go there and try to find him, and in any case, since I am dressed in rags, the guards and the other servants will prevent me from approaching him. Furthermore, dressed as I am, the king will not recognize me. I have only one alternative: to stand outside the palace and cry out from the depths of my heart, 'My beloved, merciful, forgiving master and father, please forgive my sins and crimes; have mercy on me; cease your anger against me and eradicate my sins and my guilt. Have pity on me so that I can come before you again.'"

This is what the servant did, and the king, indeed, was merciful. He received the servant kindly, forgave all his sins and crimes, and raised him to a higher rank than the other servants so that he would constantly be in attendance before him. The king did this because he recognized that the servant's heart was filled with love for him, a love so rare and so intense that the servant had abandoned everything else and risked his soul by coming before him—negating his own existence, as it were, because of the great love for the king that was burning in his heart.

The same thing applies to the penitent sinner. He abandoned God to do ugly, wicked deeds. When he repents his evil ways and regrets having drawn away from God and removed himself from eternal life, he realizes that his indulgence of his passions has made him so impure, earthly, and material that he cannot approach God's magnificence, and then his soul cries out from deep inside him. Just as it says in the Psalm, "Out of the depths have I called Thee, O Lord" (Psalms 130:1), he laments from the depths of his heart, risking his soul and negating his own existence. Now he can ascend to a higher degree than the completely righteous person. The completely righteous person worships God through the Torah and the commandments, and in his worship ascends the steps slowly, one at a time, in accordance with the merits of his worship. The penitent ascends to a higher plane before the essence of the Creator because he endangered his soul and cried out to God from the depths of his heart, risking himself and negating his own existence.

Thus the divine emanations coming downward from God are like the emanations going upward from the penitent toward God. They emanate divine light and sustenance from the Creator's essence over the penitent, in a degree high above what the completely righteous can receive. The righteous cannot reach such a degree because the divine emanation they receive is in proportion to the merits of their worship.

(Source: *Kedushat Levi, Likutim*)

1. Repentance frequently symbolizes Binah, the third sefirah.
2. The talmudic interpretation arises from the similarity between the Hebrew words for "defiled" (*nitmetei*) and "dumb" (*nitamtem*).

FASTING AND SORROW

If you feel a desire to fast, you should not prevent yourself from doing so, even though worshiping God in joy is better than worshiping in the sorrowful mood brought on by mortification of the flesh.[1] Each of us knows his own heart and soul, and if someone feels a need to fast, it is obvious that he has his reasons. In this, as in many other things, some people have to be more severe with themselves than others in order to protect their souls.

(Source: *Zava'at Ha-Rivash*, 12)

1. Literally: *sigufim*, religious practices which include an element of mortification of the flesh. Hasidism in general opposed these practices, even though some of them were based on the authority of the kabbalists of Safed. Fasting, however, presented a different problem, because at certain times it is a commandment. The author's general attitude toward fasting is evident in this passage, though it deals with the exception, when fasting is permitted.

THE DANGERS OF SORROW (I)

Sometimes the evil inclination[1] tries to lead us astray by telling us that something we have done is a grave sin when it was really just a minor transgression or perhaps not even a sin at all. It does this to make us sorrowful, because sorrow will prevent us from carrying out our assigned task of worshiping the Creator.

If you understand that the evil inclination's real purpose is to trick you into ceasing your worship of God, you will be able to resist its deceptions, telling it outright that you do not care about the transgression it is mentioning. Furthermore, even if you really did commit a small sin, the Creator prefers that you ignore it and worship Him joyously rather than sorrowfully.

The rule here is an important one. Your worship is not for your own sake but to bring joy to God, and God will not be angry if you ignore some small sin in order to prevent your worship from being interrupted. In fact, one of the major rules pertaining to the worship of the Creator is to do everything possible to keep yourself from sinking into sorrow. You should worship in joy. Weeping is very bad unless it results from happiness.

(Source: *Zava'at Ha-Rivash*)
1. *Yetzer ha-ra*, the evil power in the human soul.

THE DANGERS OF SORROW (II)

Do not let a fear that you are performing the precepts improperly frighten you into being overly punctilious.[1] Such fears are induced by the evil desires within you, which intend thereby to bring you into a state of sorrow so that you cannot worship the Creator properly.

Even if you have sinned, do not prolong your sorrow; if you do, your worshiping will stop. Let yourself experience some remorse for the sin, and then, if you really regret the sin and are determined never to repeat it, return to the joy of worshiping the Creator.

Do not be sad if you are unable to perform some precept properly. Instead, bear in mind that the Creator, who knows all your thoughts and feelings, knows that you wanted to perform it properly but could not.

Strengthen yourself by rejoicing in your Creator. Also, remember the verse that says, "It is time for the Lord to work; they have made void Thy law" (Psalms 119:126).[2] This means that the performance of some commandments entails a small element of transgression. In such cases, ignore the evil desires that want to prevent you from doing the commandment and answer as follows:

"My whole intention in doing this commandment is to bring pleasure to the Creator." If you say this, the evil desires will leave you, with God's help. But even so, do not decide for yourself whether or not to perform the commandment. And remember: everything I have written here is a basic rule, more precious than gold; even the details are basic rules.

(Source: *Zava'at Ha-Rivash*)

1. That is, in the performance of religious commandments and precepts, not day-to-day activities.
2. Compare B. Berakhot 55a.

JOY

God's supreme will decided to create all the worlds for Israel, who are called "beginning,"[1] so that they would receive the Torah and the yoke of the kingdom of heaven. The process of creating all the spiritual worlds concluded with the practical commandments. When someone performs one of these commandments with all his might and all his spiritual qualities, awakening himself to the joy that is inherent in the commandment, he awakens all the worlds with his joy, and it is as if he had added to the divine family and caused the worlds to ascend toward the supreme will with his own presence inside them. By this means he causes the divine emanation to return and descend from world to world until it reaches the most lowly worlds.

When we stand up to pray we should be moved by the joy of the commandment, for joy is the man's supreme spiritual quality, and the joy of a commandment is the supreme *yihad*.[2]

(Source: *Pri Ez: Emor*)

1. See above, "The Purpose of Creation," pp. 43–44.
2. This practice causes supreme union in the divine world (see Introduction).

PEACE

Our fathers of blessed memory said: "The characteristic of Aaron the priest is to love peace and pursue peace, to love people and draw them to the Torah" (Mishnah Avot 1:12). The expression "pursue peace" is a difficult one and requires an explanation, because "pursuing" generally means "fighting," and that sense of the word would be impossible here.

The difficulty can be explained by referring to a principle I learned from my grandfather of blessed memory, the Besht. When a patient is seriously ill, an expert physician has the right to prescribe the necessary medication even if it is potentially dangerous. Someone who knows less, however, does not have the same right, because he might make a mistake and kill the patient.

This is the key to understanding what our sages of blessed memory meant. As is well known, Aaron used to intercede whenever people were quarreling, telling each one that the other wanted to make up, and mediating between them until peace was restored. The characteristic of "drawing them near the Torah" was closely related to this, because the quarreling people would regret their quarrel when they realized that the high priest himself had to go to the trouble of interceding with each of them in order to mediate a peaceful resolution of their differences, as he always did. So they would be ashamed of what they had done and would regret it and would repent for their wicked ways, and then they would draw near the Torah.

All this applies to people who recognized how lowly they were in comparison to Aaron and felt honored by his speaking with them. But there were also fools and rogues who did not acknowledge their own lowlinessness and cared nothing about Aaron's troubling himself on their behalf, since in their stupidity his speaking with them seemed perfectly fitting. How can such persons be drawn near to the Torah and God's worship?

In such cases Aaron changed his tactics. He pursued the person, fighting with him, overcoming him, and humbling him, forcing him to recognize his own lowliness and lack of merit. Once this was done, Aaron was able to make peace between the person and those he had quarreled with, and also between the person and his father in heaven, thus drawing him near to the Torah. Our sages hinted at this when they said: "loves peace and pursues peace,"[1] for it was sometimes necessary for Aaron to be a pursuer in order to mediate for peace, as we have explained.

Even though it is not normally a pious trait to pursue a member of the people of Israel, Aaron the priest had the right to do this. All of Aaron's deeds were intended for the glory of the holy name, and everything he did was in fulfillment of God's will, not his own. Aaron understood that special circumstances occasion special methods, and in order to achieve peace he sometimes altered one of his usual modes of behavior. This is exactly what we learned from the parable referred to above.

(Source: *Degel Mahane Ephraim: Aharey*)
1. In Hebrew, *rodef* means to pursue an enemy in battle.

THE DAY OF JUDGMENT

Many of our people do not understand God's ways and works, and thus do not know how to make up for their sins and draw His good will. They fast and stay up all night praying. Such practices are very important, of course, and should not be neglected, but I wish these people would do the same things all year and not just now, during the Ten Days of Penitence, when it is more necessary. The right course to follow is one in which fasting helps you in the great effort of concentrating your thoughts—where the fear of judgment makes you hate food, so that you cannot eat, and sleep escapes your eyes, so that you cannot sleep even when your head is resting on a pillow.

Let me illustrate with a parable. Once upon a time a mortal king appointed one of his servants governor of a province. No one in the province could move a hand or a foot without the servant's permission, and all the silver and gold in the province had to be paid into the king's treasury. At the end of the year, on a day specified by the king, the servant had to bring the money to the palace and give a full account of everything that had taken place that year. According to the king's law, anyone who failed to protect the royal interests and observe the king's commandments, so preventing any harm to the king, had to pay with his head.

Now it is obvious that a servant whom a king has appointed governor and judge of a whole province will take extra care not to do anything against the king's will, and he will follow the law in every particular. He will not use even a penny of the money in the royal treasury for his own purposes. Since it is natural to be willing to give up anything to preserve one's own life, and the servant fears that the king will kill him if he does wrong, he will protect the king's interests more carefully than his own. Before he spends even one cent for his own needs, he will think long and hard whether the outlay is justified, for on the day of reckoning even a tiny sum may loom quite large.

The servant follows this course all year, but his fear increases as the specified date approaches. Day and night he organizes his thoughts and prepares his account books. Because he is concentrating so intently on the accounts, he loses his appetite and cannot sleep. He is so fearful about his impending meeting with the king that the finest delicacies and the most comfortable bed would not tempt him. His record must be completely clean, and he must be able to account for every detail without making an error, as is proper when reporting to a king.

Take this to heart and understand that what is true of the servant applies even more to the period of divine good will that extends from the beginning of the month of Elul until the day of judgment. This thirty-day period is alloted to us to make an accounting for the passing year—how you spent every day, hour, and minute; what work you did for your king. Time was created—days, hours, and minutes—so that man could worship God every day and hour in the way appropriate for that unit of time.

By doing so, man has the power to uplift the fragmented units of time to the divine sphere, where they can be reunited, and to bring them to the treasury of the King of kings. But when someone misuses his hours and minutes by fulfilling his animal desires and forgetting the Creator of the world, he will pay the king with his head, because he wasted the king's hours and minutes on his personal needs instead of bringing them to God's holy treasury.

(Source: *Or Ha-Meir*: Homily for Rosh Hashanah)

THE SHOFAR (I)

"Shall the horn be blown in a city and the people not tremble?" (Amos 3:6). To understand this verse, imagine a city whose citizens fear an attack and have posted a lookout in a tower to stand guard. The lookout sees the enemy approaching and sounds the alarm; shouting in a loud voice, he warns the citizens to organize their defenses because the enemy has come to plunder their city. When they hear this warning, the city's rich men are overcome by terror.

Their houses are filled with gold, silver, fine clothing, and possessions of every kind, and they fear that the enemy will take it all, leaving them with nothing. The city's poor, however, do not share this fear. Their houses are empty and they have no property to worry about, so they are not frightened by the prospect of enemy soldiers searching for plunder.[1]

We find, therefore, that if the lookout gives a reason for everyone to fear the enemy, the citizens are split into two groups— the rich are frightened, while the poor continue as always. But if the lookout simply sounds the alarm without giving any special reason to fear the enemy, shouting "Alas, the enemy is approaching," then everyone becomes frightened, rich and poor alike, because a simple warning means that their lives are threatened as well as their property, heaven forbid, and since the threat of death applies equally to everyone, the enemy may slaughter all the mothers and children.

From this a preacher who admonishes and instructs people should learn that everyone is different. No person is exactly like any other, because everyone's circumstances are different, and everyone lacks something different. If the preacher addresses his admonishments only to some of the people, in accordance with their special needs and problems, the others will not listen to him, concluding that they are not at fault in respect to the subject of his admonishment. The preacher has to address and guide the people in a way that applies to all of them.

That is why the sages instruct us to sound the shofar now, at the beginning of the month of Elul, in a simple voice, equal for every member of the people of Israel, rich and poor together, for the simple voice of the shofar conveys a message of mortal danger for all, and each person, regardless of his special needs or status, evokes his heart within him. Then all the people will be afraid, even the lowliest and the poorest in Torah and good works.

(Source: *Or Ha-Meir:* Homily for Rosh Hashanah)
1. The Hebrew text parallels II Samuel 12:3.

THE SHOFAR (II)

"O clap your hands, all ye peoples, shout unto God with the voice of triumph" (Psalms 47:2). The meaning of this verse is made clear by a parable. A king's beloved servants approach him to ask for something, but they are awed by his greatness and afraid to speak, lest they make a mistake and an evil servant use it against them. So they remain silent, hinting at what they want, and the king grants their request.

It is the same on Rosh Hashanah, when we, the people of Israel, are uplifted before God. Great fear overcomes us, and we are afraid to speak in God's presence lest we make some small mistake, heaven forbid, that Satan can use against us. So we shout without speaking—with the sound of the shofar, a simple sound, a cry from the depths of the heart. And our Creator, may He be blessed, who sees into our hearts and knows all that is hidden, grants our request.

(Source: *Kedushat Levi: Rosh Hashanah*)

HAPPINESS AND SACRIFICE

When you are troubled, heaven forbid, do not be unhappy for selfish reasons but because your problem, whatever it may be, is preventing you from worshiping the Creator as He ought to be worshiped. The Creator is pleased by unhappiness resulting from an inability to worship Him. We find an allusion to this idea in the talmudic passage stating that the Messiah's birthday is the ninth of Av (Mishnah Berakhot 2:4), the very day when all Israel are in mourning, their hearts aflame because of the destruction of the Temple. When the Temple was still in existence, the Creator derived great pleasure from our worship there and from the high priest's worship and from all the sacrifices, for as it says in the Torah, these were not a source of sorrow but "an offering made by fire, of a sweet savor unto the Lord" (Leviticus 1:13). In the days of the Temple, Israel lived in security and peace. Nowadays Israel should be sad only because it can no longer fulfill the Creator's wishes by giving Him the pleasure He enjoyed when the Temple was standing.

The same idea applies when something good happens to you, such as when the Creator provides you with a good livelihood or any other worldly benefit. You must connect these benefits with the Creator, so that your reason for being happy is not a selfish one but because they make it possible for you to worship Him properly.

This explanation can help us to understand the full meaning of the word "sacrifice." By "sacrificing" something, we are "bringing it near"[1]—that is, uplifting material benefits and animal pleasures to the blessed Creator, as was explained above.

To sum up: When God promises you some material favor, be happy not because of the selfish advantages deriving from the favor, but because it will enable you to worship the Creator in the right and proper way.

(Source: *Kedushat Levi: Lech Lecha*)

1. Hebrew *korban* ("sacrifice") has the same root as *hakravah* ("to bring near").

THE BENEDICTION ON FOOD

When you take a fruit or any other food in your hand and recite the benediction "Blessed art thou, O God" with intention, your mentioning the holy name awakens the spark of divine life by which the fruit was originally created. Everything was created by the power of the holy name. Since an element is awakened when it come into contact with a similar element, the benediction awakens the element of divine life in the fruit, the element which is the food of the soul. This applies to all the permitted and kosher foods, since God commanded us to uplift them from a material existence to a spiritual existence.

(Source: *Keter Shem Tov* I)

THE WICKED NEIGHBOR

It says in the Ethics of the Fathers that one should "draw away from a wicked neighbor" (Avot 1:7). This teaches us that it is easier to achieve the Holy Spirit in our time, a time of exile, than it was in the days when the Temple was still standing. To understand this, consider how difficult it would be to approach a king in his royal palace, as compared to when he is traveling through the countryside. While he is on the road or at an inn, anyone can approach him, even a simple farm lad who would never be permitted to enter the palace. In the same way, God will immediately inspire and dwell within someone who thinks about communion with God now, in our time of exile. For this reason, it is important to draw away from evil desires and evil thoughts, so as not to be separated from God. Whatever one does should be for the honor of God's name. Thus, "draw away from a wicked neighbor" means: draw away all evil from God, who dwells within you.[1]

(Source: *Maggid Devarav Le-Ya'akov*, chap. 49)

1. Hebrew *shakhen*, "neighbor," also means "dweller" or "resident." The Maggid's homiletical interpretation is: Keep all evil away from God, who is dwelling within you. He is within you even if you are ignorant and of lowly religious status, because He is in exile, "traveling through the countryside," and thus in close contact with everyone.

THE DANGER OF EVIL IN OTHERS

He who tries to draw other people to God's worship must make sure that he is not himself overcome by the evil powers of the people he redeems. The best way to avoid this danger is by using the divine aspect of judgment. In other words, he should constantly observe and judge himself, evaluating all of his own acts to determine whether he has done right or wrong. He should continually admonish and chastise himself whenever he does something wrong. The power of the divine aspect of judgment will set his heart aflame with an intense enthusiam that will burn out all the evil powers and prevent them from taking hold within him. Thus he will overcome the powers and also prevent them from taking hold of the souls whom he has drawn to the worship of God.

(Source: *Kitzur Likutey Moharan* 59a)

MONEY AND THE DEVIL

When someone performs a commandment without spending money—that is, when he refuses to spend money in order to perform it—that commandment was not performed properly, because cause it does not contain the element of faith. But when someone so loves performing a commandment that he does not care what it costs, and spends whatever is necessary, that stage is called faith, because faith is revealed by money. A person who conquers his desire for money may encounter the face of holiness.

Some people are obsessed with desire for money. No matter how much they have, it is never enough, and despite their wealth, they are unhappy, depressed, and worried. As the saying goes, "He who has more riches worries more" (Mishnah Avot 2:7). Money can shorten their life and spoil their days, for, as physicians will attest, nothing is more harmful than worry and sorrow. A person so obsessed with wealth is connected with the devil, with false gods, and with death—with the sorrow derived from false gods, also called sin, because it turns everything into wickedness and sin.

Those who hold fast to the desire for wealth are always in debt because they are ruled by their desire. They are never rich enough and continually borrow from others. They think they are rich, but when they die, they die in great debt. Even if they do not die actually owing money to others, they are still in debt with regard to their desire, for it is the devil who desires great riches. With your own eyes you can see that those who earn a good living, not to mention those who are really rich and influential, are continually involved in the race to make more money, no matter how difficult and dangerous it may be, going on lengthy journeys, facing the dangers and hardships of the road, and making desperate efforts to acquire more money, as if there were a great debt hanging over their heads that had to be paid no matter what. But the debt is really owed to their own desires and to a false god, the devil, who is always involved in a great desire for more money. Thus, such people are in debt all their lives, and they die in debt—a debt to their desire, a debt which is so infinitely large that it can never be paid.

(Source: *Kitzur Likutey Moharan* 23:10–11)

SABBATH (JOY)

The meaning of the three Sabbath meals and the festival meals is clear, but it can also be demonstrated by a parable I heard from my teacher, the Besht.

Once upon a time a prince was sent to a far-off village inhabited by humble people of little merit. After a while the prince received a letter from his father, the king. He wanted to enjoy the letter and be happy, but he was afraid that the villagers would laugh at him, saying, "Why is this day different from any other day? What reason do you have for being so happy?" Finally the prince decided on a course of action. He called all the villagers together and plied them with wine and spirits. Once the liquor had made the villagers happy and distracted them, the prince was able to get off by himself and enjoy his father's letter.

The meaning of this parable is clear. The soul is the beloved only daughter of the blessed King of kings. The Sabbath is like a love letter from father to daughter, but despite the pleasure it brings, the soul is unable to enjoy it because she is ashamed of the body, which is like a crude villager. Therefore the Torah commanded us to let the body enjoy itself on the Sabbath and festivals, and then, when the body is happy because of its physical pleasures, the soul has an opportunity to enjoy the happiness of communion with God.

This explanation should suffice. The moral of the parable teaches us that the body should enjoy the physical pleasures of the Sabbath and festivals to the extent necessary to enable the prince— that is, the soul—to enjoy the pleasures of its Father in heaven and to be happy with Him.

(Source: *Toledot Ya'akov Yosef: Tavo*)

THE REWARDS OF WORSHIP

The following parable will clarify my explanation of this matter.[1] Once upon a time two men entered into a partnership with each other. One of the partners became very rich. The other remained poor, but unlike the rich partner, he followed the way of Torah. After a while, when the two partners met again, the rich one, in accordance with the terms of their agreement, gave a sum of money to the poor one. The poor man soon lost the money and returned to his partner. The rich man wanted to give him some more money, but the poor man refused it, saying: "I'd be better off if you would tell me how you became rich; maybe I can do the same thing." The rich man replied: "Don't think you can be rich in both this world and the next world. If you want to be rich here, forget about the Torah."

When the poor man heard this, he decided to abandon the Torah and devote himself to business and making money. It did not work, however, so he went back to the rich man, who now said: "You failed because you left the Torah with intentions of becoming rich. You can only succeed if you leave it for better or worse, in riches or in poverty."

The poor man took the rich man's advice, but his business ventures still failed to work out. He went to see the rich man again, and this time he was told: "You left the Torah for better or worse, but you really hoped you would become rich, and that is why you failed. The truth is, nothing will do for you and nothing will help you."

The meaning of this parable also applies to the opposite situation. When you perform deeds that are good and just, you must not do so in order to receive a reward. As the sages said, "You should behave like servants who work without pay" (Mishnah Avot 1:3). The reward will be given anyway, if it was not your intention to receive it.

(Source: *Toledot Ya'akov Yosef: Bereshit*)

1. The "matter" referred to, which is discussed in the previous passage in *Toledot Ya'akov Yosef*, is the trials the righteous have to suffer in this world on account of the wicked, who are used as an instrument of God.

TWO TYPES OF COMMUNION

There are different opinions about the problem of communion. Some define communion as what happens when a person who is praying extends the pronunciation of one word of the prayer for a long time so as not to separate himself from the word. Others define communion as what happens when a person, by performing one of the commandments or studying the Torah, turns his body into a servant of the soul, the soul into a servant of the spirit, the spirit into a servant of the neshamah, and the neshamah into a servant of the light of the Shekhinah over his head. [1] It is as if the light spreads and envelops him, causing him to rejoice and tremble in fear at one and the same time.

(Source: Keter Shem Tov I)

    1. Medieval Jewish psychology recognized five psychic forces in man, but most discussions only concern the first three. Of these, *nefesh* ("soul") is the lowest, *ruah* ("spirit") is the second, and *neshamah* is the highest. "Servant" here translates *la'asot kiseh*, literally "to make something a chair to the other" (i.e., to make subservient to a higher spiritual force).

SECRECY

You should know how to perform your duties in secret, so that no one realizes you are practicing Hasidut,[1] but if you want to reach a very high degree, you must perform your deeds openly. If you do not practice them openly, like the other members of the community, and try to be a Hasid only internally, you may be influenced to conform to the ways of society, and then you will end up practicing the wrong way even if you started out in a good way.[2]

In the beginning, when you want to pray, you should fear God, because this is the open gate for those who want to approach Him. Say to yourself: "With whom do I want to achieve communion? With the Creator who created all the worlds by speaking, who gives them existence and life." If you observe God's greatness and loftiness,[3] you will be able to enter the divine worlds.

(Source: Zava'at Ha-Rivash)

    1. Hasidut here does not refer to the Hasidic movement, but is used in its traditional sense to denote devotional practices over and above what is required by Jewish law.

    2. In other words, even if one begins conforming to conventional patterns of behavior for a good reason—in order to keep his adherence to Hasidism a secret—there is a danger that he may end up doing what other people do without any higher motive.

    3. *Yir'at ha-romemut*, "the fear of [God's] loftiness" is the opposite of bad fear, "fear of punishment."

SOLITUDE

If you want to engage in solitary worship, do it in the company of a friend, because it is dangerous to be alone. Together in the same room, each of you can independently practice his own solitude with the blessed Creator.

Someone who is in a state of communion with God can occasionally practice solitude even in a house full of people.

One may sometimes fall from the state of communion because of his own needs—that is, because God knows that he needs a respite. A fall may also be caused by the surrounding community. In such cases the fall is but a step toward a new ascent, enabling the worshiper to achieve a very high degree. We know this from the verse that says, "He will guide us eternally" (Psalms 48:15), which is to be understood in the light of two other verses, "And Abram went down to Egypt" (Genesis 12:10) and "And Abram went up out of Egypt" (Genesis 13:1); Abram represents the soul, and Egypt refers to the evil powers.

(Source: Zava'at Ha-Rivash)

ATARAXY (I)[1]

"I have set the Lord always before me" (Psalm 16:8). "I have set" comes from the word *hishtavut*.[2] To someone who practices *hishtavut*, everything that happens is of equal significance, regardless of whether it results in his being praised or despised. He has the same attitude of indifference toward everything else, including the foods he eats. Everything is of equal significance to him because his evil desire[3] has been completely removed. Whatever happens, he will take the attitude that it comes from God and if God has seen fit to do it, he too should accept it. Similarly, all his acts will be motivated for the sake of heaven, and from his standpoint, the outcome will not make any difference. To achieve such a state of indifference is a religious attainment of a very high order.

We must worship God with all our might, because everything is necessary,[4] and God, may He be blessed, wants to be worshiped in all possible ways. In other words, when you are walking and talking with other people and cannot study the Torah, practice communion with God and work to achieve the divine unity.[5] Similarly, when you are on a journey and cannot pray or study in your usual way, worship God in other ways, and do not feel sorry about this because God wants to be worshiped in all possible ways. In fact, it was for the very purpose of making you worship Him in this particular different way that you had to take the journey or transact business with other people.[6]

In all such cases the rule is as follows: "Commit thy works unto the Lord, and thy thoughts shall be established" (Proverbs 16:3). This is a very important rule. It means that whatever happens to you happens because God wants it to happen. You should ask God to make the things that happen to you be things that He knows are good for you, and not things that human beings, with their limited perceptions, think are good for you, because what you think is good may well be bad. In regard to all your problems and needs, trust in God.

(Source: *Zava'at Ha-Rivash*)

1. G. Scholem (*Major Trends In Jewish Mysticism*, pp. 96f.) uses the Greek philosophical term *ataraxy* (meaning the absence of passion, complete imperturbability) to describe the ideas about complete indifference to one's fate in this world, voiced by such Jewish thinkers as Rabbi Bahya Ibn Paqudah, Rabbi Isaac of Acre, and the Hasidim of Ashkenaz (not the Hasidic movement treated in this book but a pietist circle in medieval Germany). As in the passage here, this idea is often expressed by the word *hishtavut*, from the root *shaveh*, "equal"; in other words, to make everything seem equal.

2. The homily is based on the similarity in sound between *shaveh*, *hishtavut*, and *shiviti*, "I have set."

3. *Yetzer ha-ra*.

4. The Hebrew text has the word *le-zorech*, "necessary," but it is probably an abbreviation for *le-zorech gavohah*, "it is necessary for God." In other words, one should worship God in all ways, because they are needed above, needed by God.

5. *Le-yahed yihuddim*, to do spiritual or practical things intended to bring God and the Shekhinah together.

6. Here ataraxy has been transferred from the human realm to the divine realm and then back to the human realm. It makes no difference to God how He is worshiped, so man should worship Him any way he can, recognizing that God is responsible for the "accidents" of life that make him change his mode of worship.

ATARAXY (II)

The principle of *hishtavut* is important. It means that you should not care whether people consider you to be ignorant or learned in the whole Torah. Constant communion with God the Creator is what makes this possible, because when you are occupied with the problem of achieving communion, you are so busy establishing your connection with God that you have no time to think about such lowly things.

Whatever you do should be intended solely to cause pleasure to your Creator, and not to fulfill your own needs, however small.

Do not think that being able to worship God with communion makes you better than your friend. All living things were created to worship God, and you are no better than any other creature. God gave your friend the same mind He gave you, so how are you better than the lowliest worm? Even the worm worships the Creator with all its might and all its mind, and man, after all, is nothing but a worm, as shown by the verse that says, "But I am a worm, and no man" (Psalms 22:7)).[1] If God had not given you a mind, your worship would be no better than the worm's worship. Thus you are no better than a worm, and certainly no better than any other human being.

Always bear in mind that you are a worm. You are no more important than the other small creatures. They are, as it were, your friends in this world—they were all created, and they all have only the ability that the Creator gave them.

(Source: *Zava'at Ha-Rivash*)

1. See also Job 25:6, Isaiah 14.11.

CHARITY AND TRUTH

Charity is connected with truth because it is an aspect of truth. Truth is unity and oneness; truth is only one, because "before one what can you count?" (Sefer Yetzirah 1:7). If there were a second, the one would not really be one. Thus truth is one. When something is true, there is only one true thing that can be said—the truth itself; but many different lies can be told about the same thing.

That is why God, the Torah, and Israel are one and the same.[1] God is truth, and His Torah is true, and Israel is truth, and since all of them are true, they are all one, because the truth cannot be divided or differentiated. As the prophet says, "For I the Lord change not; and ye, O sons of Jacob, are not consumed" (Malachi 3:6). God is true and never changes, heaven forbid; changes can only occur among those who receive from God, because change occurs in accordance with the recipient,[2] but God never changes. In the same way, the sun is only one power, but its effects seem to differ in different recipients. Depending on the recipient's response, the sun may seem to cause melting, hardening, cooling, heating, or other effects, but all these reactions are really caused by the recipients themselves. For example, wax melts when the sun shines on it, but this happens because wax is not really hard and has the property of melting. The same applies to all of the sun's other effects. But the sun itself is one power, and it never changes.

Charity is the aspect of the sun and of truth, as was stated above, and as indicated by the verse that says: "But unto you that fear My name shall the sun of righteousness[3] arise" (Malachi 3:20). This is what our sages of blessed memory meant when they said: "When a man needs charity, his face changes color" (B. Berakhot 6b). Charity causes many changes, but only because of the nature of the recipients. Charity itself, which is an aspect of truth, and an aspect of the sun, is a stable, unchanging power.

(Source: *Likutey Moharan* I, chap. 251)

1. This famous expression, appearing frequently in Hasidic literature, is usually presented as a quotation from the Zohar but was actually formulated much later. See I. Tishby, in *Kiryat Sefer*, vol. 50 (1975), pp. 480–492, 668–674.

2. In other words, the change is caused by the differences within the recipients, according to their different natures.

3. Hebrew *zedakah*, which means "charity" as well as "righteousness."

FAITH AND REASON

The phrase "Our God and the God of our fathers" is included in our prayers because there are two types of belief in God. Some people believe in God because it is a tradition handed down by their fathers; their faith is very strong. Other people have achieved faith through their own reasoning. Each approach has advantages and disadvantages. The first type of believer is very strong in his faith; he cannot be persuaded to give it up even if he is bombarded with rational arguments that disprove it, heaven forbid, partly because of the strength of his faith, but also because he has never been trained to reason and therefore is not susceptible to rational argumentation. On the other hand, his faith has no rational basis and is only the result of a reliance on the authority of other people. The second kind of believer has come to know the Creator by the strength of his own reasoning, and thus his faith is very strong and his love of God is complete. On the other hand, since he is susceptible to rational argumentation, it is often quite easy to persuade him that his faith is groundless by presenting him with rational proofs that contradict it, heaven forbid.

He who has the characteristics of both approaches is superior to everyone else. He trusts the tradition of his fathers but came to the faith by his own independent reasoning. Faith of this kind is complete and good, and because of this we say "Our God and the God of our fathers" in our prayer. "Our God" refers to what has been learned by independent reasoning, and "the God of our fathers" refers to the tradition that has been handed down to us.

(Source: *Keter Shem Tov* I)

ON THE STUDY OF PHILOSOPHY

Rabbi Nahman often spoke about books of philosophy, warning us[1] in the strongest terms possible that reading them, studying them, or even looking into them, heaven forbid, is prohibited. He explained that this prohibition is of crucial importance because such books confuse the mind by bombarding it with foreign ideas that contradict our holy Torah. Furthermore, he said, the authors of these books deny the existence of demons even though this belief is upheld by the holy sages of the Talmud.[2] Philosophy is prohibited all the more, he added, because we now have the holy Zohar and the divinely revealed[3] writings of Rabbi Isaac Luria, may his memory be blessed, and of the Besht, may his memory be blessed, to encourage us to serve God in the right way.

Therefore, anyone who is concerned about his own welfare should avoid the works of philosophy written by some of the ancient scholars, such as the biblical interpretations included in the *Mikraot Gedolot*,[4] as well as certain similar works that need not be named. Even the *Akedah* should not be studied,[5] though it is a kosher book, because it quotes philosophers and some of the problems they discussed. The same goes for the section entitled "Shaar ha-Yihud" in the *Ha-Levavot*[6] and the *Ikkarim*[7] and the explanation of the basic terms of logic by Maimonides, as well as his *Guide for the Perplexed*,[8] and the writings of other authors of a similar bent. All of these works, without exception, are absolutely forbidden. We are not allowed to study them because they confuse and injure the faithful. Happy is he who knows nothing about these works and walks the path of simplicity. These works are not part of the heritage of Jacob.[9]

. . . Whenever our rabbi talked about these books, he emphasized the importance of the prohibition against studying them. He warned us never to look at works of philosophy and always to be on guard against them. This prohibition, he said, applied especially to works written by philosophers in our own time. Run from those books to save your soul, he said, lest you go to hell and lose your share in the world to come, heaven forbid.

(Source: *Shivhey Moharan:* On Philosophy, sec. 1)

1. The speaker is Rabbi Nathan, Rabbi Nahman's closest disciple.

2. This issue was raised during the controversy concerning Maimonides' philosophical works in the thirteenth century. While Maimonides condemned witchcraft and astrology and certainly did not believe in demons, he did not explicitly deny their existence. Thus, his opponents based their arguments against him on a misinterpretation of his discussion of demons.

3. Literally: "based on the holy spirit" (*ruah ha-kodesh*).

4. *Mikraot Gedolot*, a compendium that includes the text of the Bible together with the commentaries of some of the best-known exegetes, among them Rabbi David Kimhi (thirteenth century) and Rabbi Abraham Ibn Ezra (twelfth century), both of whom used philosophical methodology in formulating their interpretations.

5. The *Akedat Yizhak* of Rabbi Isaac Arama (fifteenth century). Rabbi Nathan's description here is accurate: Arama opposed the philosophers but often quoted them.

6. *Hovot Ha-Levavot* by Rabbi Bahya Ibn Paqudah (Spain, eleventh century) was one of the best-known and most widely read books on Jewish ethics. Its first chapter, "Shaar ha-Yihud," deals with the philosophical question of the unity of God.

7. *Sefer Ha-Ikkarim* ("The Book of Dogma") by Rabbi Joseph Albo (Spain, fourteenth century).

8. The *Treatise on Logic* was one of Maimonides' earliest works; the *Guide* was his magnum opus. Both were severely criticized in the thirteenth century and later.

9. See Jeremiah 10:16.

❧

THE INFLUENCE OF THE *GUIDE*

Rabbi Nahman said that you can tell whether someone has studied the *Guide for the Perplexed* by looking at his face, because anyone who studies the *Guide* loses the image of God, the face of holiness, and thus his own face changes for the worse. Anyone can see that those who study the *Guide* and similar books become heretics and are suspected of violating all the commandments of the Torah. Like all philosophical works, the *Guide* uproots a person from Judaism and our holy Torah, and from God, and thus he is lost forever.

I [Rabbi Nathan] have spoken with several pious people who studied philosophical works, and every one of them said outright that he was sorry he had ever done so and wished he did not know what he had learned from these books. They all testified that the best course is to keep as far as possible from philosophy. Happy is he who steers clear of philosophy and strengthens his adherence to the pure faith of Judaism as we have received it from our fathers, believing as all Jews believe, without dependence on philosophy or any other such nonsense.

(Source: *Shivhey Moharan:* On Philosophy, sec. 3)

THE THREAT OF SECULAR STUDIES

The government once enacted some laws that were threatening to Jews. One of these laws, it was reported, required Jewish children to learn sciences and languages, God forbid. Our rabbi of blessed memory ordered a public fast because of this threat and urged everyone to shout and cry to God. The new law, he explained, was more dangerous than all our other troubles, because it could lead to the complete abolition of our religion. Anyone who began with secular studies would end up leaving religion altogether, unless God had mercy on the remnant of Israel and saved the few survivors. Our rabbi of blessed memory also said: "Woe to us, that we are not thinking about how to save our children and the generations to come from the evil waters that threaten to drown the whole world, heaven forbid—the evil waters of science and languages and philosophy, which are spreading in our day because of our sins."

(Source: *Shivhey Moharan:* On Philosophy, sec. 12)

RABBI NAHMAN'S STUDY OF PHILOSOPHY

There is a mystical meaning to the fact that Rabbi Nahman of blessed memory occasionally read books of philosophy, and it is the same as the meaning of the Israelites having to walk in the desert, the dwelling-place of Satan. The Holy Zohar tells us that Israel trampled Satan by walking in the desert. Books of philosophy are like the desert, and Rabbi Nahman was doing the same thing when he browsed through them. It is important to understand this, but as we have already explained, the rest of us are completely forbidden to look into such books.

(Source: *Shivhey Moharan:* On Philosophy, sec. 6)

SOURCES

The Besht's Epistle

A letter by the Besht, written in 1750 to his brother-in-law, Rabbi Gershon of Kutov, who was living in Eretz Yisrael. One of the very few authentic documents by the Besht, this letter has been the subject of considerable controversy. It was first printed as an addendum to the *Ben Porat Yosef* (Koretz, 1781), whose author, Rabbi Ya'akov Yosef, claimed that the letter had never actually been sent and remained in his possession. Intense scholarly discussion has focused on various aspects of the Besht's letter, especially in regard to its implications for an understanding of the messianic element in the Besht's teachings and in Hasidism generally. For a recent study of the letter, see A. Rubinstein's paper in *Sinai* 67 (1970): 120–139; see also I. Tishby in *Zion* 32 (1967): 29–33; B.Z. Dinur, *Between Generations* (Hebrew) (Jerusalem, 1955), pp. 181–227; and G. Scholem, *The Messianic Idea in Judaism* (New York, 1971), pp. 176–202.

Degel Mahane Ephraim

("The Banner of the Camp of Ephraim")

A collection of homilies by Rabbi Moshe Ephraim of Sedlikow, the grandson of the Besht. Edited by the author's son; first printed in Koretz in 1811 and frequently reprinted. The homilies in this collection, which follow the annual cycle of Torah lections, with some additions, contain important traditions that Rabbi Ephraim received from his grandfather, whom he frequently quotes, and thus this work is one of the most reliable sources for an understanding of early Hasidic thought.

Hayay Moharan

("The Life of Our Teacher Rabbi Nahman")

An extensive collection of the sayings of Rabbi Nahman of Bratslav, together with biographical information, accounts of the circumstances in which some of his sermons and tales were delivered, and a thematic arrangement of his conversations. Collected by his disciple, Rabbi Nathan of Nemirov. First printed in Lemberg in 1874 and frequently reprinted. Some parts of this work appeared earlier in different forms; for its publishing history, see S. Dubnow, *History of Hasidism* (Hebrew) (Tel Aviv, 1960), pp. 382–383, and G. Scholem's bibliography of the literature of the Bratslav movement, *These are the Names* (Hebrew) (Jerusalem, 1928). The *Hayay Moharan* has two parts: the first, beginning with biographical material about Rabbi Nahman, is entitled *Hayay Moharan;* the second is entitled *Shivhey Moharan ve-Sihot Moharan* ("The Praises and Discussions of Our Teacher Rabbi Nahman"). The materials included in the book were put into writing by Rabbi Nathan, but most of it is in the form of direct quotations of Rabbi Nahman. The probability that the quotations are quite accurate is demonstrated by the fact that Rabbi Nathan sometimes had to add explanatory comments to make Rabbi Nahman's ideas conform to the basic ideas of the movement. This would not have been necessary if he had felt free to alter the conversations he recorded. A discussion of several important subjects in this book will be found in the studies by J. Weiss and M. Prickaz listed below under the heading *Likutey Moharan.*

Igrot Ba'al Ha-Tania
("The Epistles of the Author of the *Tania* and His Contemporaries")
A major scholarly collection of the letters of Rabbi Shneur Zalman of Lyady, the founder of Habad Hasidism and author of the *Tania.* Included are many documents concerning Rabbi Shneur Zalman's life and teachings, including his letter about visits to the Zaddik (excerpted above pp. 94–96), as well as letters sent to him by Rabbi Menaham Mendel of Vitebsk, Rabbi Abraham of Kalish, and other contemporaries. The collection was published in Jerusalem in 1953, together with a detailed bibliography on the early development of Habad Hasidism.

Kedushat Levi
("The Sanctity of Levi")
A major homiletical work by Rabbi Levi Yitshak of Berditchev, one of the greatest Hasidic teachers and a leading disciple of Rabbi Dov Baer, the Maggid of Mezherich. First printed in Slavitta in 1798 and enlarged in many subsequent editions. The *Kedushat Levi* contains sermons for all the festivals and the weekly Torah lections. It is unquestionably one of the finest works of early Hasidic literature, but for some reason has been almost totally neglected by scholars. See S. Dubnow, *History of Hasidism* (Hebrew), pp. 193–199; S.A.

Horodetzki, *Hasidism and the Hasidim* (Hebrew), vol. 2, pp. 73–96.

Keter Shem Tov
("The Crown of [Rabbi Israel] Shem Tov")
One of the earliest Hasidic homiletical collections. Attributed to the Besht, edited by Rabbi Aharon ben Zevi Hirsch of Apta, and published in two parts in Zolkiev in 1794. Intended to satisfy the need for a trustworthy collection of the Besht's teachings, the *Keter Shem Tov* includes materials about the Besht as well as popular narrative elements from his sermons. It is made of mainly up matter derived from the works of Rabbi Ya'akov Yosef of Polonnoye but also includes selections from the homilies of Rabbi Dov Baer, the Maggid of Mezherich, and from the *Likkutim Yekarim*, an early collection. A description and structural analysis of the *Keter Shem Tov* will be found in G. Nigal's study in *Sinai* 79 (1976): 132–146. (Nigal treats the stories in this collection as "a basic source for Hasidic narrative literature," a very strange conclusion since stories and parables of the same kind, treated in much the same way, abound in countless works of pre-Hasidic ethical and homiletical literature.)

Kitzur Likutey Moharan
("The Shorter *Likutey Moharan*")
An abridged version of the *Likutey Moharan* (see below), retaining the basic ideological and theological elements of each sermon in the larger work but omitting the homiletical apparatus. Edited by Rabbi Nathan of Nemirov and first printed in Mogilev in 1811. As a popular but authentic version of Rabbi Nahman's teachings, designed to appeal to a larger audience than the original work, this book is an invaluable tool for understanding the essential doctrines of Bratslav Hasidism.

Likutey Moharan
("Collected [Sermons] of Our Teacher Rabbi Nahman")
The collected sermons of Rabbi Nahman of Bratslav, edited by his disciple, Rabbi Nathan of Nemirov. The first part was printed in Ostraha in 1808, during Rabbi Nahman's lifetime; the second, in Mogilev in 1811, shortly after his death. There have been many subsequent printings with various supplements. For the publishing history, see G. Scholem, *These are the Names* (Hebrew) (Jerusalem, 1928), pp. 12–15. The *Likutey Moharan* is the basic text of Bratslav Hasidism and one of the major literary products of the Hasidic

movement. For major recent studies of Rabbi Nahman's life and teachings, together with detailed bibliographies on all aspects of Bratslav Hasidism, see M. Piekarz, *Bratslav Hasidism* (Hebrew) (Jerusalem: Bialik Institute, 1972), and J. Weiss, *Studies in Bratslav Hasidism* (Hebrew), edited by M. Pierkarz (Jerusalem, Bialik Institute, 1974).

Maggid Devarav Le'Ya'akov
("Preachings to the People of Jacob")
The earliest and most important collection of sermons by Rabbi Dov Baer, the Maggid of Mezherich. Edited by Rabbi Shlomo of Lazk, one of his disciples. First printed in Koretz in 1781 and reprinted several times, this book is the only major Hasidic work to be published in a critical scholarly edition based on a comparison of various manuscripts and printed sources; see the edition by Rivkah Shatz-Uffenheimer (Jerusalem: Magnes Press, 1976). A detailed study of the Maggid's Hasidic doctrine will be found in R. Shatz-Uffenheimer's book, *Quietistic Elements in Eighteenth-Century Hasidic Thought* (Hebrew) (Jerusalem: Magnes Press, 1968). Other important studies of the Maggid's thought were published by the late Professor J. Weiss, among them: "Via Passiva in Early Hasidism," *Journal of Jewish Studies* 11 (1960); "The Kavvanah of Prayer in Early Hasidism," *Journal of Jewish Studies* 9 (1958); and "The Great Maggid's Theory of Contemplative Magic," *Hebrew Union College Annual* 31 (1960).

Noam Elimelech
("The Pleasures of Elimelech")
A collection of homilies on the festivals and the weekly Torah lections by Rabbi Elimelech of Lyzhansk, one of the foremost disciples of Rabbi Dov Baer, the Maggid of Mezherich. First printed in Lemberg in 1788 and frequently reprinted. One of the major products of the third generation of Hasidism, the period when the doctrine of the Zaddik became a living reality, this work is regarded as the fundamental treatment of the doctrine in its mature form. Studies of the Zaddik doctrine based on the *Noam Elimelech* will be found in R. Shatz-Uffenheimer's "On the Essence of the Zaddik in Hasidism" (Hebrew) *Molad* 18 (1960): 365–378, and in G. Nigal's Hebrew University Ph.D. dissertation (1971), "Hasidic Doctrine in the Writings of Rabbi Elimelech of Lizensk and His Disciples" (Hebrew).

Or Ha-Meir
("The Burning Light")
A major homiletical work on the weekly Torah lections by Rabbi Ze'ev Wolf of Zhitomir, one of the foremost disciples of Rabbi Dov Baer, the Maggid of Mezherich. First printed in Koretz in 1798, shortly after the author's death. Unlike many other disciples of the Maggid, Rabbi Ze'ev Wolf did not establish a Zaddik dynasty and did not personally influence subsequent Hasidic communities, but his book, which provides an original view of the religious and theological ideas that characterized the movement in its early stages, became one of the basic Hasidic texts. Very little has been written about Rabbi Ze'ev Wolf. See I. Tishby in *Zion* 32 (1967): 41–45.

Peri Ha-Aretz
("The Fruit of the Land [of Israel]")
A collection of homilies on some of the weekly Torah lections by Rabbi Menahem Mendel of Vitebsk, one of the most prominent disciples of Rabbi Dov Baer, the Maggid of Mezherich. First printed in Kopust in 1814, Rabbi Menahem Mendel's homilies reflect the Maggid's views but give more emphasis to kabbalistic elements and the doctrine of the Zaddik than is evident in the Maggid's extant writings. Rabbi Menahem Mendel was one of the disciples of the Maggid who emigrated to Eretz Yisrael in 1777, establishing a Hasidic community in Safed and, later, in Tiberias. Several of the letters he wrote from the Galilee are included in *Peri Ha-Aretz*. An edition of these letters is included D. Z. Hilman's collection of the letters of Rabbi Shneur Zalman and his contemporaries, *Igrot Ba'al Ha-Tania* (Jerusalem, 1953); see above.

Peri Ez
("The Fruit of the Tree")
A brief collection of homilies by Rabbi Menahem Mendel of Vitebsk, supplementing the *Peri Ha-Aretz* (see above). The materials in this book, which amplify and explain some of Rabbi Menahem Mendel's kabbalistic and Hasidic ideas, were collected and published by his disciples. It is an essential supplement to the *Peri Ha-Aretz*.

Shivhey Moharan
(See above, *Hayay Moharan*).

Toledot Ya'akov Yosef

The first printed Hasidic book and the most extensive collection of sermons by Rabbi Ya'akov Yosef of Polonnoye, containing homilies on the weekly Torah lections and covering all the main themes of Hasidic theology and ethics. First printed in Koretz in 1780 and reprinted several times; the title is derived from Genesis 37:2, in accordance with the custom of including the author's name in the title of his book. Rabbi Ya'akov Yosef frequently quotes sayings of the Besht, his teacher, and thus this work is the earliest and best source for the teachings of the founder of Hasidism. Other Hasidic teachers of the first generation are quoted as well, thus enabling us to reconstruct, to some extent, the spiritual climate in which the Besht lived and preached. For one such reconstruction, see J. Weiss, "The Emergence of the Hasidic Way" (Hebrew), *Zion* 16 (1951): 46–105. Important studies of this book and of Rabbi Ya'akov Yosef's writings in general will be found in S. H. Dresner, *The Zaddik* (New York, 1974); G. Nigal, *Leader and Community* (Hebrew) (Jerusalem, 1962); and G. Nigal's anthology of Rabbi Ya'akov Yosef's works, *Doctrines of the Author of the Toledot* (Hebrew) (Jerusalem, 1974).

Yosher Divrey Emet

("True and Just Words")

A collection of homilies, letters, and short theological treatises by Rabbi Meshulam Feibush Heller of Zborez, a disciple of Rabbi Menahem Mendel of Premishlan, himself a leading disciple of the Besht and the Maggid. First printed in Munkacs in 1905 but contains much material that was written in the 1870's, the decade following the death of the Great Maggid. This work is extremely important for an understanding of theological developments in early Hasidism because its author, following Rabbi Menahem Mendel, was critical in his treatment of some of the most widely accepted Hasidic ideas, such as the doctrine of the uplifting of evil desires. See I. Tishby's discussion of the theology of this work in *Hebrew Encyclopaedia*, vol. 17, pp. 788–789.

Zava'at Ha-Rivash

("The Testament of Rabbi Israel Ba'al Shem")

A collection of short homiletical pericopes on problems pertaining to worship in the Hasidic manner, especially in regard to communion with God but also treating related subjects, such as intentionality in prayer, study, joy, sorrow, etc. The attribution of this work to the Besht reflects the traditional practice of ascribing pseudepigraphical "testaments" to great scholars, a custom which apparently began in the thirteenth century with the testaments attributed to Maimonides and Rabbi Judah the Pious. Many of the homilies in this collection have counterparts, and probably their sources, in the sermons of Rabbi Dov Baer, the Maggid of Mezherich, and there can be little doubt that the ideas in the work reflect the views of his school. The *Zava'at Ha-Rivash* was one of the main targets of the Mitnagid anti-Hasidic polemic and was translated into Russian in order to demonstrate the wickedness of the Hasidic movement to the government authorities.

SUGGESTIONS FOR FURTHER READING

Although numerous books and articles have been published on the Hasidic stories, and several anthologies of Hasidic "literature" are readily available, surprisingly little first-rate material is to be found in English. The brief list below is meant to direct the student to the most authoritative of such works; in their pages further guidance will be found to more advanced studies, many in languages other than English, and several of them already referred to in the notes.

Band, Arnold, *Nahman of Bratslav: The Tales* (New York, 1978).

Buber, Martin, *The Origin and Meaning of Hasidism* (New York, 1960).

Green, Arthur, "The Zaddik as Axis Mundi in Later Judaism," *Journal of the Academy of Religion* 45 (1977): 327–347.

_____, *Tormented Master: A Life of Rabbi Nahman of Bratslav* University, Ala., 1979).

Jacobs, Louis, *Hasidic Prayer* (London, 1972).

Maimon, Solomon, *An Autobiography* (New York, 1947).

Scholem, Gershom, *Major Trends in Jewish Mysticism* (New York, 1954), pp. 325–350 and bibliography, pp. 436–438, 440.

_____, *The Messianic Idea in Judaism* (New York, 1971), pp. 176–250.

Weiss, Joseph, "A Circle of Pneumatics in Pre-Hasidism," *Journal of Jewish Studies* 8 (1957): 199–213.

_____, "Contemplative Mysticism and 'Faith' in Early Hasidism," *Journal of Jewish Studies* 4 (1952): 19–29.

_____, "Rabbi Abraham Kalisker's Concept of Communion," *Journal of Jewish Studies* 6 (1955): 87–99.

————, "The Kavvanoth of Prayer in Early Hasidism," *Journal of Jewish Studies* 9 (1958): 163–192.

————, "Via Passiva in Early Hasidism," *Journal of Jewish Studies* 11 (1960): 137–156.

INDEX